ROSE CRAFTS

ROSE CRAFTS

Using fresh and dried roses in crafts,
gifts and displays

GILLY LOVE

HERMES
HOUSE

First published in 1998 by Hermes House

Hermes House is an imprint of
Anness Publishing Limited
Hermes House
88–89 Blackfriars Road
London SE1 8HA

This edition published in the USA by Hermes House
Anness Publishing Inc., 27 West 20th Street, New York, NY 10011;
(800) 354-9657

A CIP catalogue record for this book is available from the British Library

ISBN 1 84038 086 1

Publisher: Joanna Lorenz
Editorial Manager: Helen Sudell
Editorial Assistant: Emma Gray
Designer: Bet Ayer

The publishers would like to thank the following people for designing the projects in this book:
Fiona Barnett, Penny Boylan, Andi Clevely, Stephanie Donaldson, Kally Ellis, Tessa Evelegh,
Lucinda Ganderton, Christine Kingdom, Terence Moore, Ercole Moroni, Emma Petitt,
Katherine Richmond, Isabel Stanley, Liz Trigg, Sally Walton, Stewart Walton and Pamela Westland.
The publishers would like to credit the following photographers: James Duncan, John Freeman, Michelle Garrett,
Nelson Hargreaves, Debbie Patterson, Graham Rae and Peter Williams.

Previously published as part of a larger compendium,
The Ultimate Rose Book

Printed and bound in Singapore

1 3 5 7 9 10 8 6 4 2

CONTENTS

BASIC TECHNIQUES – PRESERVING ROSES

DRYING ROSES

Roses have been dried for as long as they have been cultivated; their petals have been used in potpourri or the whole stems in decorative arrangements when the fresh flowers were scarce. The Elizabethans preserved roses by immersing them completely in dry sand and keeping them warm until all the moisture had been drawn out. In Victorian times, when houses were heated with open coal fires, which shortened the lives of fresh blooms, intricate dried arrangements were painstakingly created and then covered in glass domes to keep them dust-free. These rather tortured, contrived designs have long since lost their appeal in preference for looser, more natural arrangements and contemporary designs using dried flowers have gained a new popularity.

There are three principal ways of drying roses: in the air, in a microwave oven and using a desiccant. The latest commercial method is freeze-drying. This successful technique was originally developed as a means to store penicillin and blood plasma during the Second World War. It requires specialized freezers so it is no use putting a bunch of roses in a domestic model. The process can take up to two weeks and is therefore very expensive but the results are stunning, producing dried roses with all their former intensity of colour and, in some cases, even preserving their perfume. Flowers or bouquets dried by this method can allegedly last for about five years before they start to fade or disintegrate.

Air-drying is the most common method and by far the cheapest as it requires no more than the cost of the roses. This method is best for rosebuds that are just about to open but

BELOW: The easiest way to dry roses is to hang them upside-down in a dark, warm and well ventilated room.

ABOVE: *Once the roses are completely dry, carefully strip off the leaves and tie the buds tightly together. Combined with a halo of dried lavender, a small posy in a terracotta pot makes a delightful gift.*

still have their bud shape. They need to be hung somewhere warm, dry and dark with good ventilation for a couple of weeks – a large airing-cupboard may be ideal. Stringing them together washing-line-style speeds up the process and prevents any moisture being trapped between the flowers, which may develop into mildew. Once they are completely dry, handle them with care as the stems are very brittle. A tight bunch of rose-buds packed together in a small terracotta pot will give added impact to the now-faded colour of the petals. A gentle blow on the lowest setting of a hair drier usually removes most of any dust.

As the flowers need to fit the radius of the turntable, microwave-drying is suitable only for arrange-ments requiring quite short stems. Lay the flowers on greaseproof paper and put into the microwave oven on the lowest setting. The roses need to be checked every minute to prevent "over-cooking".

DESICCANT-DRYING

Desiccant-drying using silica gel crystals or fine sand may be used for fully open roses.

Silica gel is available from some larger pharmacies.

1 Put 1 cm (½ in) of the crystals or sand in an airtight container and lay the rose-heads face up.

2 Cover very carefully with more sifted desiccant until every part of the flower is concealed. Then tightly seal the container and keep at room temperature for approximately seven to ten days before removing from the desiccant.

STEAMING ROSES

This simple technique can greatly improve the appearance of dried roses which are imported in large boxes with up to 25 bunches per box. Frequently, some or all of the bunches arrive at their destination rather squashed. This process will give them a new lease of life, but take care. Never try to open the very centre of the rose, which is often discoloured. The process also works very well for peonies.

2 Remove the rose from the steam and gently push back the outer petals, one by one. Do not tug at the petals or you will find them coming away in your hand.

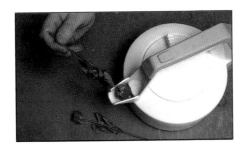

1 Bring a kettle to the boil. Hold the rose by its stem, head down-wards, in the steam for a few seconds, until the outside petals start to waver.

3 If necessary, repeat the steaming process and continue to open the petals, working from the outside towards the centre.

BASIC TECHNIQUES – WIRING ROSES

TAPING STEMS AND WIRES

Stems and wires are covered with florist's tape for three reasons. First, cut materials which have been wired can no longer take up water and covering these with tape seals in the moisture that already exists in the stem. Second, the tape conceals the wires. Third, wired dried materials are covered with florist's tape to ensure that the material does not slip out of the wired mount.

1 Hold the wired stem near its top with the end of a length of florist's tape between the thumb and index finger of your left hand (or the opposite way if you are left-handed). Hold the remainder of the length of tape at 45° to the wired stem, keeping it taut. Starting at the top of the stem, just above the wires, rotate the flower slowly, to wrap the tape around both the stem and wires, working down.

2 While taping the wired stem you may wish to add further stems, setting the flower-heads at different heights as you tape, to create "units". Finally, fasten off just above the end of the wires, by squeezing the tape against itself to stick it securely.

MAKING A STAY WIRE

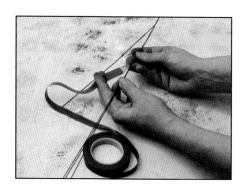

1 Group together four florist's wires, each overlapping the next by about 3 cm (1¼ in). Start taping the wires together from one end.

2 As the tape reaches the end of the first wire add another wire to the remaining three ends of wires and continue taping, and so on, adding wires and taping four together until you achieve the required length.

SINGLE LEG MOUNT

This is for wiring flowers which have a strong natural stem or where a double weight of wire is not necessary.

1 Hold the flowers or foliage between your thumb and index finger, while taking the weight of the material across the top of your hand. Position a wire behind the stem one-third up from the bottom.

2 Bend the wire ends together with one leg shorter than the other. Holding the short wire leg parallel with the stem, wrap the long wire leg around both the stem and the other wire leg. Straighten the long wire.

DOUBLE-LEG MOUNT

This is formed in the same way as the single-leg mount but extends the stem with two equal-length wire legs.

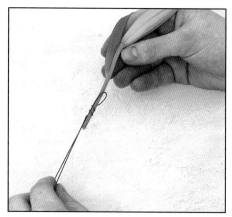

1 Hold the flower or foliage between the thumb and index finger of your left hand (or opposite way if you are left-handed) while taking the weight of the plant material across the top of your hand. Position a wire of appropriate weight and length behind the stem about one-third of the way up from the bottom. One-third of the wire should be to one side of the stem with two-thirds to the other. Bend the wire parallel to the stem. One leg will be about twice as long as the other.

Holding the shorter leg against the stem, wrap the longer leg around both stem and the other wire to secure. Straighten both legs which should now be of equal length.

WIRING A ROSE-HEAD

Roses have relatively thick, woody stems so, to make them suitable for use in intricate work the natural stem needs to be replaced with a wire stem.

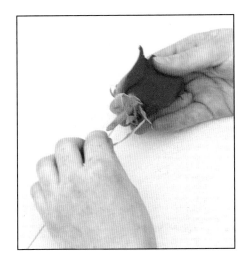

1 Cut the stem of the rose to a length of about 3 cm (1¼ in). Push one end of a florist's wire through the seed-box of the rose at the side. Holding the head of the rose in your left hand (opposite way if you are left-handed), wrap the wire firmly around and down the stem.

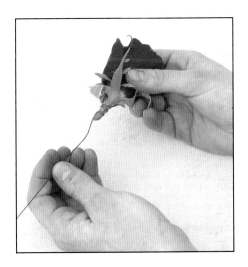

2 Straighten the remaining wire to extend the natural stem. Cover the wire and stem with florist's tape.

TYING POSIES

Simple, hand-tied posies are a very special gift and their diminutive size implies an intimacy that makes them personal and unique. The smaller the posy, the tinier and more delicate the flowers and foliage need to be. Wispy, frond-like leaves define the shape of individual flower-heads, particularly if the colours are similar, and this will give the posy more clarity.

1 Put the roses in a spiralling bunch and surround with rose leaves. Bind the flowers with raffia and trim the stems. Leaving enough ribbon to tie a bow, start winding the ribbon from the top, overlapping each twist to conceal the raffia and the stems.

2 When you reach the bottom, tuck the ribbon over the base of the stems and then wind the ribbon back up the stems.

3 When you reach the starting point, tie the ribbon in a knot before adding a bow and cut the ribbon ends on a slant to help to prevent any fraying.

ROSE CRAFTS

Roses are endlessly rewarding to work with, both as a raw material and as a design inspiration. Aspiring craftspeople of all abilities will find ideas here for creating both lovely, and useful, gifts and displays.

Rose Candles

ABOVE: *Church candles are best for decorating as they have a high proportion of beeswax and therefore burn for longer. They also soften and then harden more quickly than cheap paraffin wax.*

Candlelight is still the most romantic and flattering artificial light you can create. It enhances food, cunningly hides any dust or flaws in the room and makes faces look warm and glowing. Scented candles imbue a gentle fragrance as they burn but you should buy the better-quality examples, as cheaper versions use synthetic and often overpowering scents. A few drops of essential oil can be added to the melted pool of wax as the candle is burning for the same effect.

Aromatic burners give you the option of mixing different oils together or varying the oil if you so desire. A purpose-made dish is gently warmed by a night-light placed underneath and, as the oil evaporates, it releases its fragrance into the surrounding atmosphere. A home-made version can be improvised by placing drops of essential oil in a saucer and leaving it on top of a warm radiator.

Decorating candles is easy and the effect can be stunning. Rose-heads and leaves can be applied as decoration and each time the candle is dipped the flower or leaf is sealed more deeply into the candle. Heavier decorations take more practice: speed is crucial if it is to stick before the wax hardens.

WARNING: Never leave burning candles unattended.

MATERIALS
deep, narrow saucepan
church candle, preferably one of the shorter and fatter shapes
pressed rose-heads
selection of small silver metal shapes, such as stars
flat beads or buttons
tweezers

1 Fill the saucepan with boiling water. Dip one end of the candle into the water for 4–5 seconds. Remove from the water quickly and stick on as many of the pressed rose-heads and other decorations as you can before the wax hardens.

2 Repeat the process, turning the candle each time and not leaving it in the water for too long. A pair of tweezers may help to push the heavier items into the wax.

ROSE AND PRESSED-FLOWER GIFT WRAP

Specially made wrapping and decoration can make any present more enticing. This novel wrapping conceals an exciting surprise – pressed flowers between the wrapping paper and the box.

MATERIALS
cardboard box
tissue paper
pressed flowers
handmade paper with petals
string
sealing wax
dried roses
gift tag

RIGHT: *This idea can be adapted to suit any occasion, by varying colours and materials.*

1 Cover the box with several layers of tissue paper. Scatter pressed flowers on the top, before wrapping around the handmade paper.

2 Tie a double length of string around the parcel, finishing off with a bow. Drip sealing wax on to the string, to hold it in place.

3 Tuck three dried roses under the string and tie a gift tag on to the bow to complete the parcel.

ROSE GIFT TAGS AND BOXES

The presentation of a gift adds the finishing touch which can transform a very simple and modest item into something exciting. Careful selection of paper and trimmings show just how much thought and time has been taken for the recipient and these sentiments are always thoroughly appreciated. Even brown paper can be sprayed with an alcohol-based perfume and tied with raffia made into an exuberant bow securing a small bunch of rosebuds.

Some gifts are difficult to wrap: they are unruly shapes or so obvious in shape a degree of disguise is needed to keep the recipient guessing. Collect boxes for this purpose, such as shoe boxes. These can be covered with gift wrap and padded with layers of tissue.

Decorative rubber stamps dipped in colourful inks change plain papers into decorated wrapping. The soft ribbons found on haberdashery counters are much more luxurious than those sold in stationery shops. Gold and silver metallic stars can be stuck to plain papers for a glittery effect and also sprinkled inside the wrapping, to create an unexpected shower as the present is opened.

GIFT TAGS

MATERIALS
rose-heads or petals
rose leaves
blotting paper
flower press or heavy books
paper glue
coloured card or blank gift tag
inset paper (optional), such as
    handmade or textured
hole punch
raffia or fine string

2 After several weeks, the flowers and leaves should be completely dry, wafer-thin and very fragile. Do not be surprised if some of the original colours have either darkened or faded while drying.

1 To press rose-heads and petals, carefully place them face down on blotting paper. Cover any spaces with leaves of a similar thickness, taking care not to squash the flowers or overlap them. Cover with a layer of blotting paper and press for several weeks. If you do not have a flower press, several heavy books will work just as well.

3 Using paper glue, stick the leaves and flowers in a design on coloured card or gift tag, or for a layered effect, use a paler or white inset paper. For a rough "torn" edge, moisten the paper and gently tear the shape you want.

4 (Left) Punch a hole in the card or gift tag and thread through a long, thin piece of raffia or fine string. Use this to tie to the packet.

ABOVE: *Use dried roses to decorate wrapped presents, and pressed rose petals on your gift tags; rose motifs are also delightfully decorative.*

Gift box

A decorated gift box enhances the pleasure of a gift and also makes it intriguingly difficult to guess what is inside. Roses are a marvellous decorative motif and are particularly delightful for decorating a romantic present, especially one for Valentine's Day. The glittering stars and crescents on this gift box also make it suitable for wrapping a Christmas present.

MATERIALS
cardboard box
plain white paper
all-purpose glue
metallic stars and crescents
ribbon
dried rose-buds

1 Cover a box with plain white paper. Using all-purpose glue, squeeze dots over the top and sides and scatter metallic stars and crescents. Shake off the loose shapes.

2 Cut a piece of contrasting ribbon to length and tie around the box, knotting it in the centre of the lid.

3 (Right) Attach a tiny posy of roses to the knot with more of the same ribbon. Finish off by tying the remainder of the ribbon in a bow.

MASSED ROSE STAR DECORATION

This display has a huge visual impact of massed colour and bold shapes with the added bonus of the delicious scent of lavender.

Built within a star-shaped baking tin and using yellow and lavender colours, the display has a very contemporary appearance. It would suit a modern interior.

MATERIALS
2 blocks plastic foam for dried
flowers
knife
star-shaped baking tin
scissors
500 stems dried lavender
100 stems dried yellow roses

RIGHT: *This decoration is simple to make, although it does call for a substantial amount of roses.*

1 Cut the plastic foam so that it fits neatly into the baking tin and is recessed about 2.5 cm (1 in) down from its top. Use the tin as a template for accuracy when cutting the foam blocks.

2 Cut the lavender stems to 5 cm (2 in) and group them into fives. Push the groups into the plastic foam all around the outside edge of the star shape, to create a border of approximately 1 cm (½ in).

3 Cut the dried roses to 5 cm (2 in). Starting at the points of the star and working towards its centre, push the rose stems into the foam. All the heads should be level with the lavender flowers.

Rose Napkin Rings

Almost any type of large, preserved leaf can be used alongside roses to make these napkin rings. Preserved leaves often have dye added to the preserving liquid, which can sometimes rub off the leaf, leaving a stain. Before working with the material, give it a gentle rub with a light-coloured cloth to see if this happens (darker coloured leaves cause the most problems). Red roses are used here, but you can vary the colour to match your table setting.

MATERIALS

cobra leaves

glue gun

red roses

green moss

RIGHT: *Home-made napkin rings add a special charm to a table setting and, of course, can be made to co-ordinate with any other floral table and room decorations.*

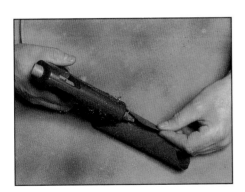

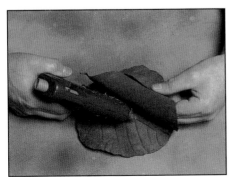

1 (Above left) Roll a leaf to form a tube, glue the edge down and hold it until it sets.

2 (Below left) Glue the tube-shaped leaf to a flat leaf along its centre spine. Choose a leaf that is about the same length as the rolled leaf.

3 (Above right) Either side of the rolled leaf, glue two red roses. If they are rather small, glue more than two or steam them to make them look larger.

4 (Below right) Trim with a little green moss, glued in place.

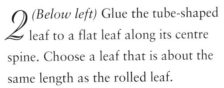

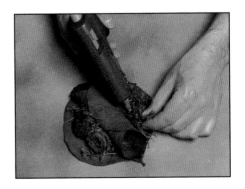

VALENTINE'S HEART CIRCLET

ABOVE: *This takes a little more effort than ordering a bunch of flowers from your florist, but that effort will be seen as a measure of your devotion.*

*I*nstead of the traditional dozen red roses, why not give the love of your life a wall-hanging decoration for Valentine's Day?

Set your heart (in this case wooden) in a circlet of dried materials full of romantic associations – red roses to demonstrate your passion, honesty to affirm the truth of your feelings and lavender for the sweetness of your love.

MATERIALS
33 heads dried red roses
scissors
silver reel wire
florist's tape
55 stems dried lavender
10 stems dried honesty
florist's wires
1 small wooden heart, on a string

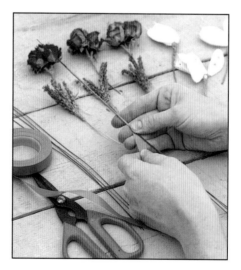

1 Cut the dried rose stems to approximately 2.5 cm (1 in) and individually double-leg mount on silver reel wires, then cover the stems with tape. Group three rose-heads together and double-leg mount on reel wire. Cover the stems with tape. Repeat the process for all the rose-heads, making in total eleven groups.

Group the dried lavender into bunches of five stems and double-leg mount on silver reel wire, then tape. Repeat the process for all the lavender, making eleven groups.

Cut pods from stems of dried honesty, group into threes and double-leg mount them on silver reel wires and tape. Make eleven groups.

Make a stay wire from florist's wires.

2 Lay a group of the honesty pods over one end of the stay wire and tape on securely. Then add, so that they just overlap, a group of lavender stems followed by a group of rose-heads, taping each group to the stay wire. Keep repeating this sequence, all the while bending the stay wire into a circle.

3 When the circle is complete, cut off any excess stay wire, leaving approximately 3 cm (1¼ in) to overlap. Then tape the two ends together through the dried flowers, to secure. Tie the string from the wooden heart on to the stay wire between the dried blooms, so that the heart hangs in the centre of the circlet.

HEART-SHAPED ROSE WREATH

This striking decoration uses a single type of rose in one colour.

MATERIALS
florist's wires
florist's tape
scissors
50 stems dried red roses
silver reel wire

1 Make a stay wire with florist's wires and tape. Form it into a heart shape about 22 cm (8¾ in) high, with the two ends of the wire meeting at its bottom point.

2 Cut the rose stems to about 2.5 cm (1 in). Double-leg mount them on silver reel wire and tape.

ABOVE: *This effective heart would make an unusual and long-lasting Valentine's Day gift.*

3 Starting at the top, tape the rose stems to the stay wire. Slightly overlap the roses to achieve a continuous line of heads, finishing at its bottom point. Starting back at the top, repeat the process around the other half of the heart. Tape the two ends of the wire together.

ROSE AND POTPOURRI GARLAND

This is a delicate and pretty garland, which uses a hop-vine ring as its base. These are fairly inexpensive and can be purchased ready-made from good florists. If you prefer, you could make your own, using vines or twigs cut when green so that they are pliable. Weave them together to form a ring and leave it to dry completely, when it will hold its shape.

MATERIALS
dried rose-heads
scissors
glue or glue gun
ready-made hop-vine or twig ring
sphagnum moss
potpourri
fir cones or woody material

ABOVE: Although garlands are usually hung on a wall or door, they can be very effective as a table decoration, provided that they are not too large. Check that there are no pieces of wire sticking out from the back.

1 Steam the heads of the roses to improve their appearance if necessary. Cut off the stems of the roses and glue the heads to the ring, some in pairs and others as single roses. Try to achieve a good balance. Next, glue hanks of moss to the ring in the gaps between the roses.

2 Now apply generous quantities of glue directly on to the ring and sprinkle on handfuls of potpourri, to cover the glue completely. Finally, add the fir cones or woody items, gluing them on to the ring singly or in pairs. Keep checking that all the material is well spaced. Work on the garland in sections and move the base ring around as you finish decorating each part.

RIGHT: Try to keep the flowers and ingredients of this garland light and delicate. No decorative trimmings are really necessary but you could, perhaps, add a rustic trailing raffia bow.

OLIVE OIL CAN ARRANGEMENT

2 Cut the dried roses so that they protrude about 10 cm (4 in) above the rim of the tin. Starting at the left-hand side of the tin, arrange a line of five tightly packed roses in the plastic foam from its front to its back. Continue arranging lines of five roses parallel to the first and closely packed across the width of the tin.

An old olive oil can may not be the first thing to spring to mind when considering a container for your dried flower arrangement, but the bright reds, yellows and greens of this tin make it an attractive option.

Since this container is so striking, the arrangement is kept simple, using only one type of flower and one colour. This creates an effective contemporary display.

ABOVE: If you come across a nice container, however unlikely, remember it may be just right for a floral display. If you are using dried flowers it does not need to be watertight.

MATERIALS
*1 block plastic foam for dried flowers
knife
small rectangular olive oil can
scissors
40 stems dried 'Jacaranda' roses
raffia*

1 Cut the plastic foam to fit snugly in the olive oil can, filling it to 2 cm (¾ in) down from its rim.

3 Continue adding lines of roses, until the roses are used up. Then take a small bundle of raffia about 3 cm (1¼ in) thick and twist it to make it compact. Loosely wrap the raffia around the stems of the roses just above the top of the tin and finish in a simple knot.

ROSE BUTTONHOLES AND CORSAGES

It used to be the fashion for gentlemen to present their ladies with an elaborate corsage of scented flowers to wear on a special occasion such as a grand ball. This custom is now mainly restricted to wedding guests wearing boring carnations with a sprig of asparagus fern as buttonholes. With imagination and a little skill and expenditure, though, it is quite possible to create some really attractive arrangements to wear for formal occasions, such as weddings or other special events. Traditional etiquette demands that ladies wear corsages with the flowers pointing downwards and gentlemen wear buttonholes with the flowers upright.

ABOVE: *Present buttonholes and corsages in tiny boxes protected by coloured tissue paper, to help them keep fresh until they are worn.*

GENTLEMAN'S BUTTONHOLE

MATERIALS
1 stem 'Ecstasy' rose
scissors
medium-gauge florist's wire
florist's tape
3 heads eryngium (sea holly)
3 heads lavender
2 ivy leaves

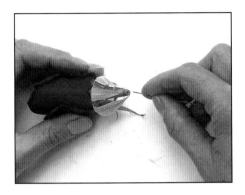

1 Assemble all the ingredients. Cut the stem off the rose about 1 cm (½ in) below the head. Push a small piece of florist's wire through the remaining stem up into the head. Check that the wire feels quite secure and not likely to become loose.

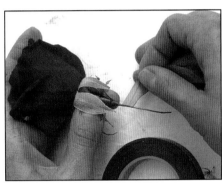

2 Pull the florist's tape so that it stretches and bind it around the stem and wire, sealing them together. Repeat this step, wiring and taping the eryngium stems and the lavender, to create two little bunches.

3 Wire the ivy leaves (see Lady's Corsage). Then arrange one individual flower with the ivy leaves so that the leaves form a flat back to the buttonhole. Ensure that the wires are completely covered.

4 To make the ivy leaves more stable, create a loop of wire at the back of the buttonhole to support each leaf.

LADY'S CORSAGE

MATERIALS
medium-gauge florist's wire
2 stems 'First Red' roses
fine silver reel wire
2 large ivy leaves and 1 smaller one
florist's tape
2 sprigs cotoneaster berries
co-ordinating ribbon, preferably wired

1 Wire the roses. Thread the fine wire through the main vein on each ivy leaf, leaving one long end.

2 Wrap the shorter wire around the stem. Wind the longer wire around the stem and other wire. Tape.

3 Add the roses and berries. Bind the stems and tie with a ribbon.

ROSE POTPOURRIS

*I*n times when personal hygiene did not exist and rubbish and worse were thrown from the most convenient window, scented flowers and plants were essential to disguise the vile odours encountered in every-day life. Dried herbs were burned in fireplaces to stave off the dreaded plague and floors were covered with branches of fragrant lavender, rosemary, sage and other aromatic "strewing" herbs. Bowls were filled with dried scented roses to sweeten the air.

The name "potpourri" means, literally, "rot-pot", and the moist method of making the mixture involves mushing together petals and spices with salt and sometimes brandy and leaving in a jar for a week. The dry method is simpler and the results look more attractive. To make quantities of potpourri, you need to grow – as well as roses – lavender, scented pelargonium (geranium), dianthus (garden pinks) and other brightly coloured flowers.

Orris root is required in both moist and dry potpourri recipes. This is a powdered root which acts as a fixative in these scented blends and is available from traditional pharmacists and herbalists.

Lay freshly picked rose petals and leaves on blotting paper or other absorbent paper, making sure that the petals are not touching. Leave to dry in a cool place where there is a good flow of air. Sprays of flowers like delphiniums need to have their individual flower-heads removed from the stem. Use only when the petals are completely dry.

ROSE AND DELPHINIUM POTPOURRI

MATERIALS
250 g (9 oz) dried scented rose petals
90 g (3½ oz) dried delphinium
*   flowers and marigold petals*
large screw-topped jar
15 ml (1 tbsp) dried mint leaves
5 ml (1 tsp) ground cloves
5 ml (1 tsp) ground cinnamon
5 ml (1 tsp) ground allspice
15 ml (1 tbsp) ground orris root
8 drops rose essential oil

1 Mix the petals and flowers together in the jar, adding the other ingredients one by one. Shake well in between each addition. Screw the lid on tightly and leave for two or three days in a dark cupboard.

ABOVE: When the petals are completely dry, they are ready to be made into potpourri.

LEFT: Petals and rose-heads need to be left somewhere cool and dry with a good air flow.

CITRUS AND ROSE-SCENTED POTPOURRI

MATERIALS
250 g (9 oz) dried scented rose petals
90 g (3½ oz) dried lavender and
*   lemon balm*
airtight container
dried grated peel of 2 large lemons
5 ml (1 tsp) ground allspice
5 ml (1 tsp) ground orris root

1 Mix the flowers and herbs together in an airtight container, add the lemon peel and leave for two to three days. Add the spice and orris root, shake well, and leave for a week, stirring occasionally.

RIGHT: The aroma of Rose and Delphinium Potpourri can be enhanced by adding a few drops of rose essential oil or rose geranium oil.

Summer Potpourri

The traditional potpourri is based on rose petals. This is because when rose petals are fresh, they have a powerful fragrance. Some of their distinctive fragrance is retained when they are dried, unlike many other perfumed flowers. Today's potpourri does not rely entirely on the fragrance of its flowers, since there is a wide range of scented oils available and this means materials can be used just for their visual qualities.

This potpourri is traditional in that it uses dried roses, but modern in that whole buds and heads have been included, instead of petals. The sea holly heads, apple slices and whole lemons are used entirely for their appearance.

MATERIALS

20 stems lavender
15 slices preserved (dried) apple
5 dried lemons
1 handful cloves
20 heads dried pale pink roses
2 handfuls dried rose-buds
1 handful hibiscus buds
10 eryngium (sea holly) heads
large glass bowl
potpourri essence
tablespoon

RIGHT: Predominantly pink and purple, the look and scent of this potpourri will enhance your home throughout the summer months.

1 Break the stems off the lavender leaving only the flower spikes.

Place all the dried ingredients in the glass bowl and mix together thoroughly. Add several drops of potpourri essence to the mixture of materials – the more you add, the stronger the scent. Stir thoroughly with a spoon to mix the scent throughout the potpourri. As the perfume weakens with time it can be topped up by the addition of a few more drops of essence.

HEART AND FLOWERS

A heart-shaped dried-flower decoration with a traditional feel of the country. The construction of the heart could not be simpler and it will last a long time, if you do not hang it in direct sunlight. This is a lovely way to preserve the best of summer's harvest of roses to enjoy throughout the winter months.

MATERIALS

4 long florist's wires
florist's tape (optional)
florist's reel wire
hay
dark green florist's spray paint
clear glue or glue gun
wide red ribbon
narrow gold ribbon
large and small dried red roses
dried hydrangea heads
scissors

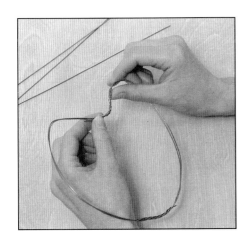

1 Form two pairs of florist's wires into a heart shape. The double thickness of the wire gives the arrangement better support. Tape or twist the ends together at the top and bottom of the heart.

2 Using reel wire, bind hay all the way around the heart, to create a firm frame about twice the thickness of a pencil. Work around the heart at least twice with the reel wire, trapping as many loose ends of hay as possible. Cut off and tie the wire, and trim any loose ends of hay. Spray the whole frame dark green and leave it to dry.

3 Glue the end of the red ribbon to the bottom of the heart and wrap it around the frame. Repeat with the gold ribbon. Tie a bow at the top with a length of gold ribbon. Cut any stems from the roses and separate the hydrangea into florets. Glue the large rose-heads near the centre and surround them with hydrangea. Put the smaller rose-heads along the top.

ABOVE: *Roses are a symbol of romance* par excellence *and so what better way to preserve some beautiful garden roses than to combine them with that other emblem of romance: the heart.*

STARFISH AND ROSE TABLE DECORATION

This is an original decoration for a large church candle, using dried rose-heads and starfish. The result is a table-centre decoration with a seaside feel. This is a simple and quick decoration to make, but is very effective nonetheless.

WARNING: Never leave burning candles unattended.

MATERIALS
9 small dried starfish
florist's wires
church candle, 13 x 23 cm (5 x 9 in)
13 cm (5 in) ring plastic foam for dried flowers
scissors
reindeer moss
40 heads dried roses

1 Double-leg mount all the starfish individually through one arm with florist's wires, to extend their overall length. Cut the wires to approximately 2.5 cm (1 in) in length and put the starfish to one side.

2 Position the candle in the centre of the plastic foam ring. Make 4.5 cm (1¾ in) long hairpins from cut lengths of florist's wires. Use these to pin the reindeer moss around the edge of the ring.

ABOVE: *The cream roses complement the colour of the candle and contrast is provided by the apricot colour and strong geometric shape of the small dried starfish.*

OPPOSITE: *Make sure that you replace the candle well before it reaches the level of the roses.*

3 Group the wired starfish into sets of three and position each group equidistant from the others around the foam ring. Push their wires into the foam to secure.

4 Cut the stems of the dried rose-heads to about 2.5 cm (1 in) and push the stems into the foam to form two continuous, tightly packed rings of flowers around the candle.

CHRISTMAS CENTREPIECE

*E*ven the humblest materials can be put together to make an elegant centrepiece. The garden shed has been raided for this one, which is made from a terracotta flowerpot and wire mesh. Fill it up with red berries, ivies and white roses for a rich, Christmassy look; or substitute seasonal flowers and foliage at any other time of the year.

MATERIALS
knife
1 block plastic foam
18 cm (7 in) terracotta pot
about 1 m (39 in) wire mesh
beeswax candle
tree ivy
white roses
red berries
variegated trailing ivy

1 Cut the plastic foam to fit in the terracotta pot and soak it in water. Push the foam in the pot.

Place the pot in the centre of a square of wire mesh. Bring the mesh up around the pot and bend it into position. Position the candle carefully in the centre of the pot. Arrange tree-ivy leaves around the candle.

2 Add a white rose as a focal point, and arrange bunches of red berries among the ivy. Add more white roses, and intersperse trailing variegated ivy among the tree ivy.

WARNING: Never leave burning candles unattended.

OPPOSITE: *The wire mesh gives a strong, curving shape that is nevertheless light and airy. Its ruggedness prevents the traditional Christmassy elements from seeming clichéd.*

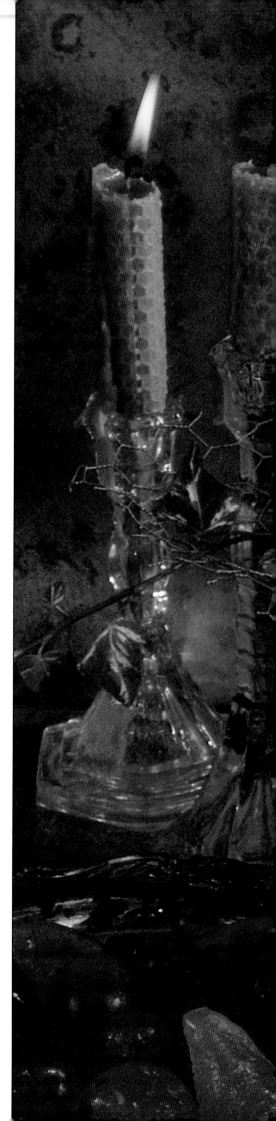

CANDLE POT WITH PERFUMED ROSES

This is a delicate and appealing design, based on a flower-filled hay collar that is secured to the top of a pot, leaving the centre free for a large candle. You could make one for each table setting at a dinner party; or, alternatively, make a few larger pots as a centrepiece, with vibrant green moss and small fruits arranged around their bases.

WARNING: Never leave burning candles unattended.

MATERIALS
large handful of hay
florist's reel wire
scissors
terracotta pot
strong, clear glue or glue gun
moss
dried rose-heads
small-leaved dried foliage, such as bupleurum
candle

OPPOSITE: *In these delightful candle pots, one shows a simple combination of pink roses and bupleurum, while the other is a mixture of large and miniature roses. With this version, add the smaller roses after filling the main gaps with bupleurum. Perfumed oil gives a wonderful lasting fragrance to the display; sprinkle a few drops of rose oil on the moss.*

1 Make the hay collar by scrunching the hay up into a sausage. Wind reel wire around it tightly at 1 cm (½ in) intervals. Measure around the inside rim of the pot before trimming its length to fit.

2 Glue the hay collar into place, so that it is stuck inside the rim of the pot as near to the top as possible. Hold it firmly in position for a few seconds, while the glue begins to harden.

3 Glue moss to the collar, so that it also covers the rim of the pot. Now you are ready to start adding flowers. Carefully cut the rose-heads from their stems, and start to glue them into position.

4 Work from one side of the pot to the other so that you keep the flowers balanced. Make sure that the hole in the centre of the pot remains large enough to take the candle. After the roses, fill any gaps with greenery. Next, place moss in the base so that it half fills the pot. Press it down firmly to form a solid base for the candle. The aim is to have as much of the candle exposed as possible.

SUMMER CANDLE-CUFF

Choose a tall, wide candle for this project, so that the cuff is large enough to apply the dried-flower materials. The candle must be at least twice the height of the cuff, so that it has plenty of room to burn without any danger of setting the hessian alight. Make sure the candle is well wrapped before the start of the project, to ensure that it is kept clean and that the hot glue will not melt the wax as it is applied to the paper base and hessian.

WARNING: Never leave burning candles unattended.

MATERIALS
scissors
thick brown paper
candle
adhesive tape
hessian
strong, clear glue or glue gun
rope
twigs
florist's wire
green moss
6 stems dried roses

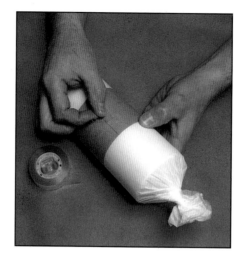

1 Cut a piece of brown paper approximately 8 cm (3¼ in) wide and long enough to wrap around your chosen candle. Tape the loose end down; you must be able to move the paper collar freely up and down the candle.

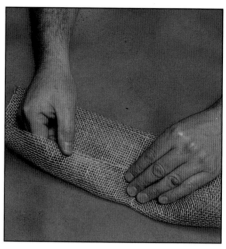

2 Cut a piece of hessian twice as wide as the paper and long enough to wrap around the candle. Fold in the two outside quarters to meet in the middle and glue them down.

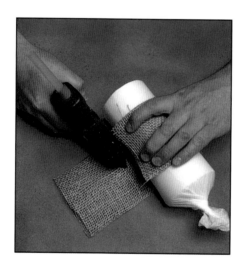

3 Lay the candle on the wrong side of the fabric and apply a little glue on either side of the candle. Wrap the fabric tightly around the candle, smoothing it to fit the paper neatly, and applying additional glue where necessary.

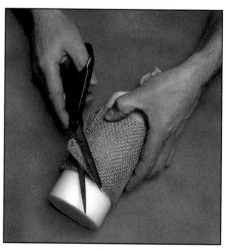

4 Trim the corners of the exposed edge and glue them down with a small dab of glue.

5 Wrap the rope around the hessian cuff once and hold it in place. Apply glue all the way around the rope, so that the glue comes into contact with both the rope and the hessian. Wrap the rope around the candle again, as close as possible to the first wrap, pushing it into the hot glue. Repeat the process until the whole of the cuff has been covered.

6 Make a small bundle of twigs and centre-wire it. Glue the bundle and some green moss to the cuff at an angle, using the moss to cover the wire that holds the twigs together. Cut the heads from the roses and glue them around the twigs.

RIGHT: *This project requires a little patience but, when you have mastered the technique, you can vary it by using different materials, such as fir cones, dried mushrooms and dried white roses for a wintry look.*

DRIED ROSE POMANDER

A pomander is generally defined as a ball of mixed aromatic substances. However, this pomander is designed more for its visual impact than its scent. It would look particularly attractive if carried by a bridesmaid, and a young child might find this easier to manage than a posy. Alternatively it can be hung in the bedroom, perhaps on the dressing-table.

MATERIALS

scissors

10 stems glycerined eucalyptus

15 cm (6 in) ball plastic foam for dried flowers

3.5 cm (1⅜ in) wide ribbon

florist's wires

30 stems dried pink roses

florist's tape

12 stems dried pale pink peonies

12 preserved (dried) apple slices

1 dried ti tree

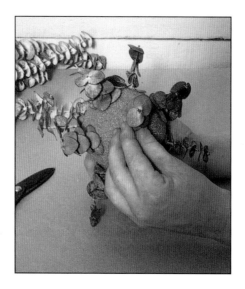

1 Cut the eucalyptus stems into approximately 10 cm (4 in) lengths. Take care to ensure that the stem ends are clean and sharp, and carefully push them into the plastic foam, distributing them evenly over its surface.

2 Cut a length of ribbon long enough to make a looped carrying handle. Make a loop in the ribbon and double-leg mount the two cut ends together on florist's wire. Push the wire firmly into the plastic foam ball, to form the carrying handle.

3 Cut the stems of the dried roses to approximately 4 cm (1½ in) and wire individually with florist's wire. Group together in threes, bind with wire and cover with tape. Cut the dried peony stems to approximately 4 cm (1½ in) and wire them individually, then tape the stems. Finally, wire the dried apple slices individually on florist's wires.

4 Push the wired peonies into the plastic foam, distributing them evenly all over the ball. Push the wired apple slices into the foam, also distributing them evenly over the ball.

5 Push the ten groups of wired roses into the foam, distributing them evenly all over. Cut the ti tree stems into 9 cm (3½ in) lengths and push into the foam to fill any gaps around the ball. Once completed, you may wish gently to reposition individual elements, in order to achieve the most pleasing effect.

ABOVE: This charming scented ball can be used as a bridesmaid's bouquet or hung in a bedroom.

ROSE AND CLOVE POMANDER

This pomander is a decadent display of rose-heads massed in a ball. But it has a secret: cloves hidden between the rose-heads give the pomander a lasting spicy perfume.

Its dramatic impact relies on the use of large quantities of tightly packed flowers, which should all be of the same type and colour.

MATERIALS

ribbon, 40 x 2.5 cm (16 x 1 in)
florist's wires
10 cm (4 in) ball plastic foam for
    dried flowers
scissors
100 stems dried roses
200 cloves

ABOVE: *Almost profligate in its use of materials, this pomander is quick to make and would be a wonderful and very special gift.*

1 Fold the ribbon in half and double-leg mount its cut ends together with a florist's wire. To form a ribbon handle, push the wires right through the plastic foam ball so that they come out of the other side, and pull the projecting wires so that the double-leg-mounted part of the ribbon is firmly embedded in the plastic foam. Turn the excess wire back into the foam.

2 (Left) Cut the stems of the roses to approximately 2.5 cm (1 in). Push the stems into the foam, to form a tightly packed circle around the base of the ribbon handle. Push a clove between each rose-head. Continue forming circles of rose-heads and cloves until the foam ball is completely covered.

ROSE-BUD AND CARDAMOM POMANDER

These rose-bud pomanders are fun to make and add a pretty touch to any room. They can be hung on a wall, or over a dressing-table mirror. When the colour has faded they can be sprayed gold to make an effective Christmas ornament.

MATERIALS
ribbon or cord for hanging
medium florist's wires
7.5 cm (3 in) ball plastic foam for
  dried flowers
scissors
small rose-buds
all-purpose glue
green cardamom pods

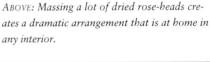
ABOVE: *Massing a lot of dried rose-heads creates a dramatic arrangement that is at home in any interior.*

1 Make a long loop with the ribbon or cord. Bind the base of the loop with wire. Leave a long end of wire, and push this through the centre of the ball and out through the other side. Trim the wire to about 2.5 cm (1 in) long, and bend the end over so that it is lost in the foam ball.

2 Stick the rose-buds into the foam by their stems. If they have no stems, use a little glue. Cover the entire ball with roses, pressing them close together to make sure that none of the foam is visible. Once the ball is completely covered, glue some green cardamom pods between the rose-buds, to give a contrast in colour and texture.

ABOVE: *Roses look delightful when used in topiary balls, but take great care when handling the flowers as the petals tend to crumble easily. When you first start to work on a ball, cut all the stems to the same length before you begin, so that it will be easier for you to achieve a perfect round shape. As you work, trim the stems and adjust the flowers so that they are all at the same height.*

ROSE-SCENTED BAGS

A translucent, gossamer fabric made into a simple bag and filled with scented rose-heads and petals is a delightfully feminine idea for a guest room. Keep the flowers lightly perfumed, by adding a few drops from a small bottle of pot-pourri refresher. Larger bags with a drawstring hung in a wardrobe will emit a faint but pleasant aroma each time the door is opened. You could make an alternative to a Christmas stocking by filling a large version with dried rose petals and tiny gifts. Choose fabric that is either extremely fine or transparent, such as organza, fine silk and chiffon, or open-weave linen or muslin, which will allow the perfumed flowers to breathe through it.

MATERIALS
outer fabric, 35 x 24 cm (14 x 9½ in)
lining fabric, 35 x 24 cm (14 x 9½ in)
dressmaker's pins
needle and matching thread
dressmaker's scissors
iron
length of co-ordinating cord, about
*   40 cm (16 in)*
adhesive tape
2 matching tassels
dried scented rose petals

OPPOSITE: A few drops of rose essential oil will refresh the petals and keep the rose bags lovely and fragrant.

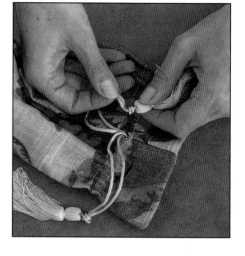

1 Lay the outer and lining fabrics one on top of the other, right sides together. Sew a seam around all four sides, leaving a 3 cm (1¼ in) gap on one side. Turn the bag through this gap, so that it is right-side out. Press all four seams and slip-stitch the small gap closed. About one-quarter of the way down the bag, run two lines of stitches across the width of the bag, about 2 cm (¾ in) apart. This is to accommodate the drawstring.

Fold the bag in half, with the right sides together. Sew up the bottom and side of the bag. Turn right-sides out and press.

2 At the side seam, make a small snip in the outer fabric, to allow the drawstring through. Take care not to cut through both layers of fabric.

Wind a piece of adhesive tape around the end of the cord, to prevent it from fraying, and feed it into the gap in the seam. Feed it all the way around the bag until it comes out at the other side through another small hole. Tie a single loop in both ends of the cord and attach a matching tassel to the end of each cord.

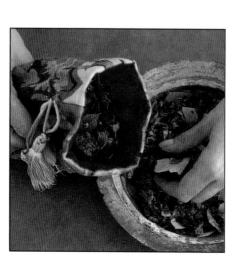

3 Fill the bag with scented rose petals. Pull the cord, to create gathers in the neck of the bag. Tie a knot to secure the bag and neaten any edges.

ROSE AND LAVENDER-SCENTED SACHETS

Scented cushions are a charming way to scent your home. They release their fragrance every time they are leaned against.

ROSE AND LAVENDER-SCENTED SACHETS

MATERIALS
50 g (2 oz) rose petals and buds
10 g (¼ oz) lavender flowers
10 g (¼ oz) oakmoss (optional)
5 bay leaves, crumbled
15 ml (1 tbsp) ground cinnamon
15 ml (1 tbsp) ground orris root
10 drops rose oil
40 cm (16 in) square muslin
needle and matching thread
30 x 60 cm (12 x 24 in) thick wadding
30 cm (12 in) square cushion cover

1 Mix all the dry ingredients in a bowl and add the rose oil.

2 Fold the muslin in half twice and seam along two sides to create a bag 20 cm (8 in) square. Fill with the aromatic mixture and stitch the opening closed.

3 (Left) Place the scented bag on the wadding and fold the wadding over the bag. Stitch around the wadding to create the pad for the cushion. Slip the scented cushion pad into the cover.

ROSE-SCENTED SACHETS

Make the sachets in the same way as Rose and Lavender-scented Sachets and then fill with the following:

MATERIALS
75 g (3 oz) scented red rose petals
25 g (1 oz) ground orris root
25 drops rose oil

LEFT: *Scented sachets are a simple, yet delight-ful gift to receive.*

OPPOSITE: *A scented cushion tucked in amongst the others on a sofa will release its delicate fragrance when it is leaned against.*

Scented Rose Cushion

Making this cushion could not be simpler – it requires no sewing at all, just a safety pin! The lace is fine enough to allow the rose scent to permeate into a clothes drawer or through a pile of pillows on a bed. Every now and then, a small amount of essential oil or pot-pourri refreshing perfume will be needed to refresh the petals. Tiny sachets can also be made from circles of the thinnest muslin or by using lace handkerchiefs.

Make a small pile of potpourri in the centre of the fabric, crushing or tearing some of the larger petals or rose-heads. Gather the fabric together and tie it securely with a fine ribbon. Small silk or fabric rose-buds or flowers can then be sewn or glued on to decorate the neck of the bag.

If you are giving a present of fine linen or lingerie, the addition of two or three rose sachets makes more of your gift.

Materials
lace or fine synthetic lace curtain
   fabric, 25 cm (10 in) square
pins
scissors
90 cm (1 yard) two colours of thin
   silk ribbon
safety pin
rose-scented potpourri

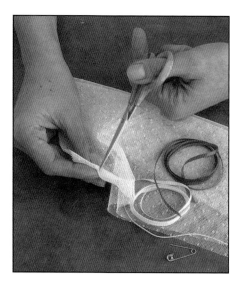

1 Fold the fabric in half and pin the edges together. Make small cuts through both pieces of fabric 2 cm (¾ in) from the edge and at small intervals all the way round.

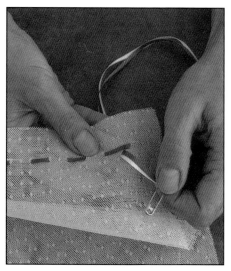

2 Attaching one end of both pieces of ribbon to the safety pin, thread it through the holes, leaving a small gap on one side of the cushion for filling with potpourri.

3 Fill the cushion with rose-scented potpourri through the small opening. Crush or tear the larger petals or rose-heads to fit through the small opening.

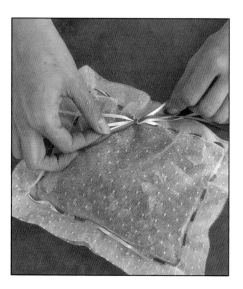

4 When the cushion is filled, continue threading the ribbon to close the gap and tie in a bow. If you pull the ribbon tight, you can give the hem a ruched effect.

OPPOSITE: *Scented sachets can be made from lace handkerchiefs that are simply tied up with a piece of ribbon.*

ROSE HAIR SLIDE

Long-lasting and resilient hair slides and bands made with fabric roses are ideal for tiny brides-maids who cannot resist putting their hands in their hair every few minutes, reserving the fresh flowers for posies or small baskets.

MATERIALS
glue gun with all-purpose glue
sticks
metal hair slide
fabric roses with leaves

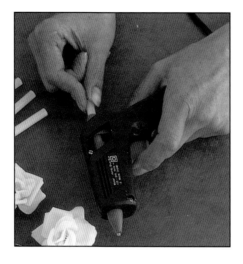

1 Always take great care with glue guns as the glue is very hot. Insert the glue stick and wait for the gun to heat up. The trigger will pull easily when the glue has melted.

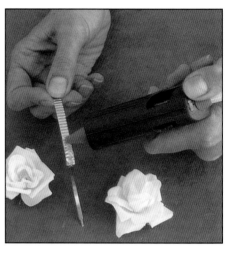

2 Squeeze an even line of glue along the top edge of the hair slide, always keeping your fingers well clear of the piping hot glue.

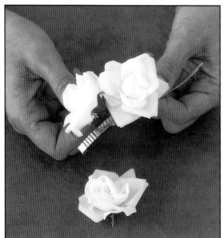

3 Stick the rose-heads to the slide pointing to alternate sides, so that their bases are completely covered.

4 Turn the slide over and add more glue to stick fabric leaves to the slide, to fill any gaps that remain.

STEMMED TARTAN ROSES

What would every gardener not give to have produced roses of such wondrous colours and lasting beauty? Fun to make and certain to be a talking point, these tartan roses can be adapted to suit many occasions. Make them the centrepiece of a festive table or use them to decorate place settings. Alternatively, you can make them part of a festive wreath or garland, or stitch a single tartan rose to a plain evening dress or evening bag.

MATERIALS
florist's wire, 20 cm (8 in)
tartan ribbon, 60 cm x 4 cm
  (24 x 1½ in)
needle and matching thread
scissors
tartan wire-edged ribbon, 30 cm x
  4 cm (12 x 1½ in)
fine florist's wire
florist's tape

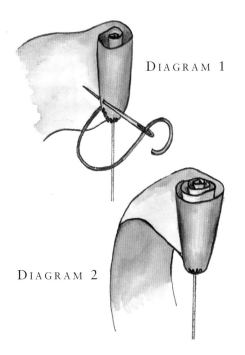

DIAGRAM 1

DIAGRAM 2

1 Bend the end of a piece of stub wire to form a hook equal in depth to the ribbon width. Holding the tartan ribbon with the cut end to the right, hook the wire through the upper right-hand corner of the ribbon, approximately 5 mm (¼ in) from the edge. Close the hook to hold the ribbon.

2 Roll the ribbon around the hook two or three times from right to left, to enclose the wire. Stitch to secure *(see diagram 1)*. Then, holding the wire stem in your right hand and the loose ribbon in your left, fold the ribbon so that it runs down parallel to the wire *(see diagram 2)*.

3 Roll the covered hook end from right to left into the fold, turning tightly at the bottom and loosely at the top until the ribbon is once again horizontal to the wire.

4 With the wire stem facing towards you, stitch the base of the rose to secure it in place.

5 Continue folding the ribbon and rolling the rose in this way, stitching the base after each fold until the desired shape and size of rose are achieved. To complete the rose, cut the ribbon squarely, fold it back neatly on to the rose and stitch lightly to hold in place *(see diagram 3)*.

6 To make the triple leaf, cut the wire-edged ribbon into three equal lengths. Cut three equal lengths of fine florist's wire and make a small loop in each about 2.5 cm (1 in) from one end.

7 Fold two corners of a piece of wire-edged ribbon down and forwards to form a triangle. Place one of the pieces of wire centrally in the triangle, with the loop on the lower selvedge and the short wire end pointing upwards. Stitch the ribbon to secure the wire in place.

DIAGRAM 3

8 Fold the lower corners of the ribbon triangle under and backwards to create a leaf shape. Gather the lower part of the leaf neatly round the long wire stem and stitch to secure in place.

9 Make two more leaves in this way. Bind the wire stems of two of the leaves with florist's tape for about 1 cm (½ in). Bind the wire stem of the third leaf for approximately 2.5 cm (1 in). Join the three leaves together at this point and continue binding around all three wires to create a single stem. Bind the stem of the tartan rose, binding in the triple leaf about 10 cm (4 in) down from the rose.

OPPOSITE: *Roses made from tartan ribbon are amusing and cheerful and would make a striking part of a contemporary Christmas table setting.*

ROSE HAIR SLIDE

Ribbon roses are surprisingly straightforward to make and can be used to trim a wide range of gift items and sewing projects. The choice of harmonizing colours in a variety of ribbon widths gives a charming posy effect to this hair accessory, which would be ideal for a young bridesmaid. A fabric-covered hair band could also be decorated with a row of flowers or a straight bar clip could be trimmed with pearls.

MATERIALS

50 x 4 cm (20 x 1½ in) cream lace
10 cm (4 in) oval hair slide
PVA glue
20 cm x 3 mm (8 x ⅛ in) pale green ribbon
20 cm x 3 mm (8 x ⅛ in) each, pale pink, dark rose pink and beige ribbon
For the roses:
needle and matching sewing threads
80 x 2.5 cm (32 x 1 in) warm beige ribbon
75 x 2.5 cm (30 x 1 in) dark rose pink ribbon
50 x 1 cm (20 x ½ in) pale pink ribbon
30 x 1 cm (12 x ½ in) cream ribbon
60 x 5 mm (24 x ¼ in) dark rose pink ribbon
30 x 5 mm (12 x ¼ in) dark pink ribbon

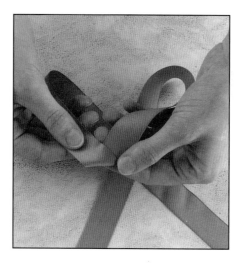

1 To make a ribbon rose, thread a needle with matching thread and have this standing by for the final step. Fold the ribbon at a right angle, two-thirds along its length, and hold in place.

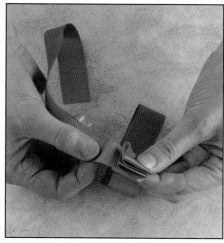

2 Pass the long end under the triangular fold and hold with your other hand. Pass the short end under, then continue to make concertina folds to the end of the ribbon.

3 Hold the two ends together, and gently grip with the thumb and forefinger of one hand. Carefully draw up the long end. This ruffles the ribbon and forms the rose petals.

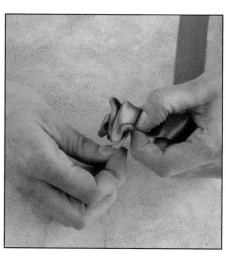

4 Still holding the rose, make several stab stitches, being sure to pass through all the layers of ribbon. Fasten off the thread and trim the ends of the ribbon.

ABOVE: Ribbon roses can be made into exquisite decorations: you could match hair accessories and trimmings for dresses.

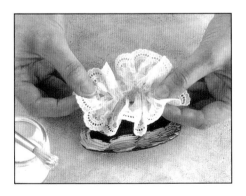

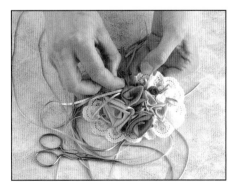

5 Gather the lace along the straight edge and draw up to fit on to the hair slide. Tucking the raw ends neatly under, glue in place with PVA glue and leave to dry.

6 Following the method given, make the roses: one warm beige, two large dark rose pink, three pale pink, two cream, one small dark rose pink, three dark pink. Arrange the roses inside the gathered lace and stick in place, one at a time, with the larger roses towards the centre of the hair slide.

7 Cut several 4 cm (1½ in) lengths of the green ribbon and stitch the ends together to form loops. Sew these between the roses along one outer edge. Make loops and streamers from the rest of the narrow ribbons and attach as shown.

VELVET ROSE COAT HANGER

Perfect for hanging up a special garment or to give as a gift, this coat hanger makes use of the luxurious texture and rich colours of velvet to recreate the charm of roses in full bloom. Ready-made fabric leaves are easily available.

MATERIALS
tape measure
wadding
dressmaking scissors
wooden coat hanger
needle and matching sewing threads
paper
pencil
green and red velvet
sewing machine
fabric leaves
matching narrow velvet ribbon

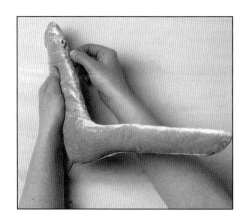

1 Cut two pieces of wadding about 30 cm (12 in) square. Wrap each arm of the hanger in wadding and sew it in place. To make the paper template, put the hanger on a sheet of paper and draw around it. Add 1.5 cm (⅝ in) all around and around the ends. Cut two pieces of green velvet to this size. With right sides together, stitch the upper edge and the rounded ends.

2 Turn right-sides out. Unpick the centre and slip the velvet over the hanger. Slip-stitch the bottom edges together.

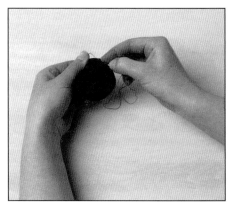

3 Cut a piece of red velvet 10 x 30 cm (4 x 12 in), fold it in half lengthways and stitch the long edge and one short edge. Turn right-sides out. Roll up the velvet from the unstitched short end, to make a rose, and secure it with a prick stitch.

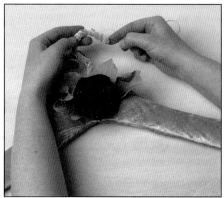

4 Stitch the rose and fabric leaves to the hanger. Wrap the ribbon around the hook and slip-stitch.

LEFT: *For your most special and treasured clothes, a decorative padded hanger will not only protect delicate fabrics but also add to the excitement of dressing up.*

RIBBONWORK CHRISTENING PILLOW

Create an heirloom gift combining the freshness of pure white cotton with the silky-soft appeal of roses and other flowers embroidered in delicate pastels. Duplicate the embroidery design on a cot quilt for a pretty but practical duo that will see service for many years. This type of ribbon embroidery is easy to work and can produce lifelike effects.

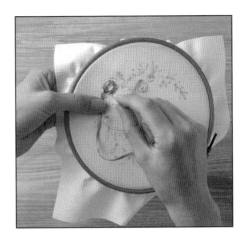

MATERIALS

tape measure

white cotton piqué, 90 x 30 cm
    (36 x 12 in)

scissors

lightweight iron-on interfacing,
    23 x 23 cm (9 x 9 in)

iron

dressmaker's carbon or vanishing
    marker pen

embroidery hoop

chenille needle

satin ribbon in pale pink, mid pink,
    dusky pink, pale mint green,
    pale lime green, pale aqua,
    1.75 m x 3 mm (2 yd x ⅛ in) of
    each

ribbon, 1.4 m x 5 mm (1½ yd x ¼ in)

narrow broderie anglaise insertion,
    1.4 m (1½ yd)

broderie anglaise edging,
    1.4 m x 7.5 cm (1½ yd x 3 in)

dressmaker's pins

needle and matching and contrasting
    threads

tapestry needle

cushion pad, 30 x 30 cm (12 x 12 in)

1 Cut a 23 x 23 cm (9 x 9 in) square of cotton piqué and iron the interfacing to one side. Transfer the garland design to the fabric, by tracing it through dressmaker's carbon or by drawing it freehand with a vanishing marker pen. Mount the fabric in an embroidery hoop. Work the roses, by stitching a star shape of four overlapping straight stitches in pale pink. With darker pink ribbon, work a circle of overlapping, slightly longer stitches around the centre to make the effect of petals.

2 Using the various shades of green ribbon, work the leaves in straight stitch and the rose-buds in lazy daisy stitch. Work a single pink straight stitch for the centre of each rose-bud and fill any spaces with small French knots. Work the rest of the garland design using a range of formal and random stitches. The photograph will act as a guide. Trim the finished piece to a 15 cm (6 in) square. Finish with a small, single-loop bow made from a piece of 5 mm (¼ in) ribbon.

3 (Left) Cut four 9 cm (3½ in) squares of cotton piqué. Cut four 15 x 9 cm (6 x 3½ in) rectangles. Cut the broderie anglaise insertion in four 9 cm (3½ in), two 15 cm (6 in) and two 33 cm (13 in) lengths. Edge one side of each square and one long side of two of the rectangles using a 1 cm (½ in) seam allowance. Sew the insertion-edged rectangles to opposite sides of the embroidered square. Sew an insertion-edged square to either end of the two remaining rectangles.

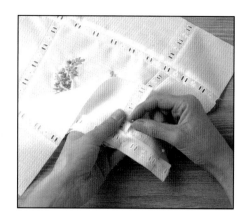

TEMPLATE

4 Use the two remaining strips of broderie anglaise insertion to join all three strips together, thus framing the embroidered square (see diagram 1). Press the seam allowance towards the central square on the wrong side.

5 Join the two ends of the broderie anglaise edging and run a gathering thread along the raw edge. Fold the edging into four equal sections, marking each quarter division with a small scissor cut. Pin each of these cuts to one corner of the pillow top, on the right side. Draw up the gathering thread to fit the cushion. Distribute the gathers evenly, allowing a little extra fullness at the corners. Pin the broderie anglaise around the outside edge so that it lies on top of the cushion. Tack and then sew in place.

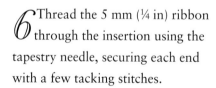

6 Thread the 5 mm (¼ in) ribbon through the insertion using the tapestry needle, securing each end with a few tacking stitches.

7 (Right) Cut a 30 cm (12 in) square of cotton piqué for the pillow back. Pin to the right side of the pillow front, ensuring that the lace is free of the seam line. Sew around three sides then turn to the right side. Insert the cushion pad and slip-stitch the fourth side closed.

DIAGRAM 1

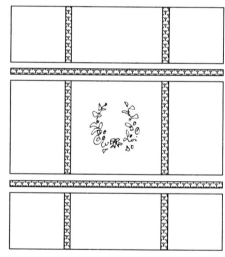

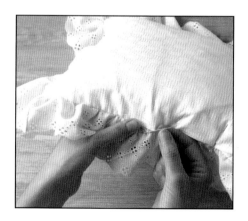

OPPOSITE: Ribbonwork roses combine with cotton piqué and broderie anglaise to make this exquisite pillow. It will be treasured for years.

SATIN-ROSE HAT DECORATION

Decorate a straw hat for a summer wedding or garden party with a vibrant rose made of satin ribbon. Use ribbons of different widths and colours to make a bunch of roses or stick to one beautiful specimen that will catch every eye.

MATERIALS
scissors
satin ribbon in 3 complementary
  shades
needle and matching sewing threads
green florist's wires
green ribbon
green crêpe paper or florist's tape

RIGHT: *Satin ribbon has all the lustre of real rose petals and a satin rose will give a plain and simple straw hat all the promise of summer but will last unfaded into the depths of winter.*

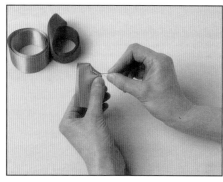

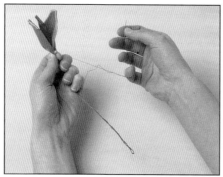

1 Make each petal separately, starting with the centre petal. Cut a piece of ribbon, about twice the width of the ribbon in length, and fold it with wrong sides together. Fold over each of the top corners twice and stitch them down invisibly. Repeat to make enough petals for a rose, using different shades and widths of ribbon.

2 Roll the centre petal around itself and secure with a stitch. Insert a stem wire into this first petal and continue to add petals around the rose, stitching them together as you go.

3 Finish the rose by binding with green ribbon, to hide the raw edges. Stitch it in place at the top, just over the base of the petals, and then gather up the lower edge neatly and stitch it securely. Bind the stem with crêpe paper or florist's tape.

OPPOSITE: *Beautiful blowsy paper roses grace a simple straw hat, turning it into something to wear for a special occasion.*

RIBBON-ROSE HAIR BAND

Choose ribbons to match a bridesmaid's outfit or a party dress. With practice, these pretty ribbon roses will be easy to make.

MATERIALS

60 cm (24 in) length of 6 cm (2¼ in) tartan ribbon
needle and matching sewing thread
scissors
2 m (2 yd) of 4 cm (1½ in) sheer green plain and gold-edged ribbons
satin-covered padded hair band
38 cm (15 in) lengths of 4 cm (1½ in) gauze and satin ribbons

2 Cut the green ribbon into 15 cm (6 in) lengths and fold them to make leaves. Sew them to the centre of the hair band and then attach the rose in the middle.

3 Make six more roses in different colours and sew them along the hair band, interspersing them with more green leaves in plain and gold-edged ribbon.

1 Make the central rose first. Fold one end of tartan ribbon at a right angle and twist it around twice, to form the centre. Secure at the bottom with a few stitches. Form the first petal by twisting the ribbon around the centre, folding it back at a right angle, so that the top edge lies across the "stalk", and catching it down with a secure stitch. Continue to wrap the ribbon around in this way, securing each petal with a stitch. Finish off firmly, by stitching through all the layers of ribbon.

ABOVE: *Ribbon roses have the advantage that you can make them in almost any colour or pattern, to suit any outfit, and they will last for a long time.*

TUDOR ROSE CUSHION

ABOVE: *The deep, glossy red of real rose petals is reflected in the silk of this cushion, which is quilted with the most classic and traditional rose motif: the Tudor rose.*

The classic Tudor rose motif is picked out in quilting lines on this vibrant silk cushion; the traditional rosy red colour is a perfect complement for the motif.

MATERIALS

tracing paper
pencil
fine black felt-tipped pen
tape measure
red silk taffeta, 100 x 90 cm (40 x 36 in)
quilter's pencil
calico, 100 x 90 cm (40 x 36 in)
dressmaker's scissors
wadding, 50 cm (20 in) square
dressmaker's pins
needle and tacking thread
sewing machine
red sewing thread
vanishing marker pen
piping cord, 1.5 m (1½ yd)
polyester stuffing

1 Trace the Tudor rose template, enlarging it as necessary. Outline the rose in black pen. Cut a 50 cm (20 in) square of silk. Lay the silk on top and trace the rose directly on to the fabric, with the quilter's pencil. Cut a 50 cm (20 in) square of calico. Layer the wadding between the calico and the silk. Tack the layers together with lines of stitches radiating from the centre. Using red thread, quilt along the outlines of the design, working from the centre out. Once complete, draw a five-sided shape around the design and trim the cushion along the lines.

2 Cut and join several 5 cm (2 in) bias strips of red silk. Press the seams open and trim them. Fold the bias strip over the piping cord and tack. Pin and tack the piping around the edge of the cushion, with the raw edges together. Machine-stitch close to the piping. Lay a square of silk and then of calico over the right side of the cushion. Pin, tack and stitch around the edges, leaving a small gap. Trim the seams and corners and turn through. Fill with polyester stuffing and slip-stitch the gap closed.

TWO-TONE ROSE SCARF

Wrap yourself in garlands of roses by stamping a silk scarf with this red and green rose pattern. Scarves are wonderfully versatile and they really can make an everyday outfit look very special – wear this one around your neck or as a sash, or you could even use it to wrap up your hair, gypsy-style. When you are not wearing your scarf, drape it over a chair or hang it on a peg, to add dashes of colour to a room.

The scarf shown here was originally cream but it was then dipped in pink dye for an attractive two-tone effect – a light-coloured scarf would work just as well.

MATERIALS
red and green fabric paint
plates
foam rollers
small rose and rose-bud stamps
silk scarf
backing paper (thin card or newspaper)

ABOVE: *Stamping produces a charmingly informal effect reminiscent of folk art techniques. This rose stamp is perfectly in tune with that informality and will cheer you just by hanging in the room!*

1 Spread the paints on the plates and run the rollers through them until evenly coated. Ink the small rose red and its leaves and the rose-bud stamp green. Stamp them on the corner and edges of the paper.

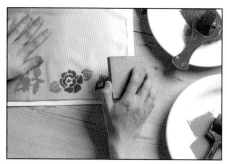

2 Slip the paper pattern under the scarf and print alternating small roses and rose-buds around the border, using the roses on the backing paper as a positioning guide.

3 Fill the middle of the scarf with two parallel rows of small roses.

BLACK ROSE VASE

The transparency of this plain glass vase creates the illusion that the black rose is floating in mid-air, somewhere above the mantelpiece. Glass is an interesting surface to stamp on because of its smoothness. The paint disperses as soon as it is applied to the glass. Have a spare piece of glass handy, so that you can practise your stamping before committing yourself to the final print. This way, you can find out exactly how much paint you need to get the desired effect.

There are now paints available called acrylic enamels. They are suitable for use on glass and ceramics and give a hard-wearing finish that stands up to non-abrasive washing.

MATERIALS
plain rectangular glass vase
kitchen cloth
black acrylic enamel paint
plate
foam roller
large rose stamp
piece of glass

1 Wash the vase, to remove any grease from the surface. Dry it thoroughly.

2 Spread some black paint on to the plate and run the roller through it, until it is evenly coated. Ink the stamp and make a test print on the glass.

3 Stamp the black rose in the centre of the vase front. Apply gentle pressure with a steady hand and remove the stamp directly, to prevent it from sliding on the slippery surface. If you are not happy with the print, wipe it off before it begins to dry, clean the glass and try again.

ABOVE: *This stamped black rose is graphic and dramatic and, used on a plain vase, would be suitable for the most modern interior.*

ART NOUVEAU ROSE BOX

Inspired by the early-20th century work of the Glasgow School of Art, this design for a simple wooden box combines swirling *art nouveau* shapes and stained-glass style roses to dramatic effect.

MATERIALS
fine-grade sandpaper
white primer paint
oval wooden craft box, with lid
soft pencil
tracing paper
thick bristle and fine hair
    paintbrushes
paint-mixing container
rose pink, green, yellow, white, black
    and blue acrylic paints
clear acrylic or crackle varnish

ABOVE: *This box decorated with roses is the perfect place to keep rose-scented potpourri.*

1 Sand and prime the box. Enlarge the template and transfer it to the lid, with a pencil and tracing paper.

2 Paint the rose petals and the leaves as solid blocks of colour.

3 Paint the stems and thorn ring; add shade to the flowers. Paint the leaf veins and outline the petals.

4 Colour-wash the rim of the lid with watered-down rose paint. Paint the box blue. Seal with varnish.

ROSE-STAMPED STATIONERY

ABOVE: *Romantic golden roses embellish inexpensive plain stationery and its box to dramatic effect. Whether you give the stationery box as a gift or use the stationery for your special letters, you will delight the recipient.*

*H*and-printed stationery sends its own message, even before you have added your greetings or invitation. This golden rose would be particularly suitable for wedding stationery, making a welcome change from mass-produced cards.

MATERIALS

tracing paper
hard and soft pencils
linoleum square
lino-cutting tools
gold paint
small paint roller
metal ruler

blank stationery, such as deckle-edged
    notepaper and envelopes
fine paintbrush
glue stick
stationery box
Japanese paper, cut into strips
ribbon

1 Trace the rose motif, enlarging it as necessary. Transfer to the linoleum. Using a narrow-grooved tool, cut out the motif, keeping your free hand behind the blade at all times. With a wide tool, cut away the excess lino. Indicate with an arrow which edge is the top, on the back.

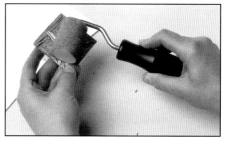

2 Ink the lino stamp with gold paint and stamp the stationery, re-inking the roller each time. Wipe away any build-up of paint.

3 Edge the envelopes, cards and the top edge of the notepaper with a fine line of gold paint. Glue the box with strips of Japanese paper. Arrange the notepaper and cards in the box. Bind the envelopes with more Japanese paper and ribbon and add them to the box. Decorate the box lid with ribbon.

ROSE-STENCILLED TABLECLOTH

Two stencils are arranged here to decorate a square tablecloth; the same motifs could be used in many different combinations and scales. Use two or three shades with each stencil shape, to achieve a rounded, three-dimensional look to the roses, leaves and branches.

MATERIALS
tracing paper
hard and soft pencils
stencil card
craft knife
cutting mat
heavy white cotton fabric, 75 cm
  (30 in) square

spray adhesive
dark pink, pale pink, yellow,
  dark green, light green and
  warm brown stencil paints
3 stencil brushes
vanishing marker pen
long ruler
set square
needle and white sewing thread

ABOVE: Stylized roses and leaves are a charming folk-art motif but, arranged in these dramatic borders, have an unexpected sophistication.

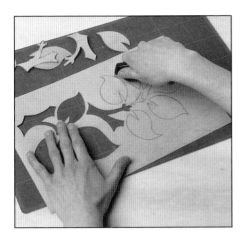

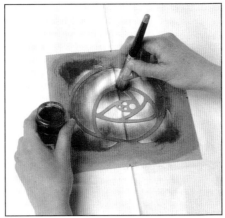

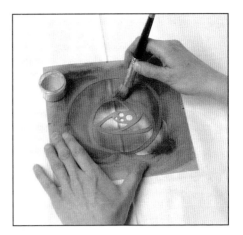

1 Enlarge the rose template so that it measures 15 cm (6 in) across. Enlarge the branch template so that it is 30 cm (12 in) long. Transfer both on to the stencil card and carefully cut out the stencils, with the knife, on the cutting mat.

2 Fold the fabric in half each way, to find the centre. Press lightly along the creases. Spray the back of the rose stencil lightly with adhesive and place it in the middle of the cloth. Start with dark pink paint in the corner petals and round the outer edge of the inner petals.

3 Fill in the rest of the petals with pale pink and colour the centre dots in yellow. Keep the brush upright and use a small circling motion to transfer the paint. Be careful not to overload the bristles. Peel off the stencil and allow the paint to dry.

4 Work a branch motif on each side of the rose, using the crease as a placement guide, to form a cross. Spray the back of the card with adhesive, as before. Stencil yellow paint in the centre of each leaf.

5 Blend dark and light green paints and finish painting the leaves.

6 Work a small amount of brown around the base of the leaves and the outside edge of the branches. Stencil a rose at the end of each branch. With a fabric marker, and using the ruler and set square to get a perfectly accurate square, draw a line about 15 cm (6 in) from each edge, so that it is on the same level as the outer edge of the roses. Stencil a rose in each corner and then work branches between the roses.

7 (Right) When the paint is quite dry, fix it according to the manufacturer's instructions. Turn under, press and stitch a narrow double hem along the outside edge.

AROMATHERAPY MASSAGE OIL

Rose essential oil is one of the most expensive and is often sold mixed with a small amount of carrier oil such as jojoba. Each essential oil has different qualities and values which a qualified aromatherapist can use to create a specific programme of holistic treatment.

Massage is one of the most effective methods of experiencing the healing properties of these oils. You can create your own massage oil by blending essential oils with a carrier oil such as pure sunflower or grapeseed. Never apply neat essential oil directly on to the skin unless under the supervision of a qualified aromatherapist. Though recommended in many books, it is also unwise to add neat essential oils to a bath as the oil may appear to disperse but will not actually do so and can therefore come in direct contact with the skin, causing an allergic reaction. Essential oils can be immensely beneficial but need to be used advisedly.

APHRODISIAC MASSAGE OIL

A light, non-greasy and fragrant oil for a sensual massage over the entire body which is relaxing and luxurious.

5 drops rose essential oil
3 drops ylang ylang essential oil
2 drops jasmine essential oil
105 ml (7 tbsp) grapeseed oil
5 ml (1 tsp) wheatgerm oil

HARMONIOUS MASSAGE OIL

The essential oils in this blend, combined together, create a harmony related to the ability to love. Rose has healing and sensual qualities; sandalwood is relaxing and sensual; clary sage, euphoric and uplifting; geranium, cleansing and refreshing; ginger, fortifying and warming.

13 drops rose essential oil
2 drops sandalwood essential oil
2 drops clary sage essential oil
3 drops geranium essential oil
3 drops ginger essential oil
20 ml (4 tsp) jojoba oil
105 ml (7 tbsp) unrefined sunflower oil

AFTER SUN SOOTHING OIL

Prolonged sun-bathing, particularly in the hottest part of the day, can have a devastating effect on the skin. It encourages premature ageing and, if you burn, it can be very painful. Prevention is, of course, better than cure, but if you are feeling tender, and providing the skin is not actually burnt and broken, this massage oil is very comforting and moisturizing.

5 drops rose essential oil
5 drops chamomile essential oil
45 ml (3 tbsp) grapeseed oil
45 ml (3 tbsp) virgin olive oil
15 ml (1 tbsp) wheatgerm oil

1 Mix several essential oils together in a base of carrier oil such as grapeseed, jojoba or sweet almond, to produce a massage oil that has specific therapeutic benefits.

2 Never exceed 1 drop of essential oil for every 20 drops of carrier oil. These oils should be purchased in dropper bottles so it is easy to be accurate when you are making up your own blends.

RIGHT: *Rose essential oil is one of the most precious and luxurious of all perfumed flower oils.*

FACIAL BEAUTY WITH ROSES

The most delicate skin on the body's surface is on the face and, though true beauty comes from within, there is nothing quite so attractive as a fresh and clear face that radiates good health. Millions are spent each year on beautifying lotions, particularly those reputed to forestall the onset of ageing. Rose essential oil is nourishing and moisturizing and 3–4 drops mixed with 20 ml (4 tsp) jojoba oil make a simple but effective facial oil to apply after the skin has been thoroughly cleansed.

ROSE CREAM CLEANSER AND FACE MASKS

This simple cleanser is mildly astringent with both soothing and cooling properties. It should be made up in small quantities and kept in the refrigerator. If you reduce the rose-water to 5 ml (1 tsp) and replace it with the honey that has been gently warmed, you have a face mask suitable for dry skin but gentle enough for sensitive faces. Adding the oatmeal, stirring well and leaving for 10 minutes produces a mask that can also be used as an exfoliating skin scrub. As with all face masks, this is most effective if used while relaxing in a bath and left on the face and neck for about 10 minutes before washing off very thoroughly.

OPPOSITE: 'Awakening' is a climbing rose with fully double blooms that flower continually through the summer.

MATERIALS
mixing bowl
spoon
105 ml (7 tbsp) triple-distilled rose-water
45 ml (3 tbsp) double cream
30 ml (2 tbsp) unblended clear honey
airtight container
30 ml (2 tbsp) fine-ground oatmeal

1 Mix the rose-water with the cream and honey and stir well. Keep in an airtight container in a cool place until ready to use. To use, smooth over the face and neck.

2 The addition of oatmeal to the honey, cream and rose-water mix makes an exfoliating face mask. Smooth over the face, avoiding eyes and sensitive areas, relax for 10 minutes, then gently rinse off.

ROSE AND CHAMOMILE FACIAL STEAM AND SKIN TONICS

Hot-water facials open the skin's pores and not only make the face feel refreshed but create a sense of well-being and relaxation.

MATERIALS
large bowl
hot water
3 drops rose essential oil
4 drops chamomile essential oil
towel
For the dry skin tonic:
75 ml (5 tbsp) triple-distilled rose-water
30 ml (2 tbsp) orange-flower water
For the oily skin tonic:
90 ml (6 tbsp) triple-distilled rose-water
30 ml (2 tbsp) witch-hazel
airtight bottles

1 Fill a bowl just wider than your face with hot water and add 3 drops rose essential oil and 4 drops chamomile essential oil.

2 Cover your head with a towel and drape it over the bowl. About 5 minutes is usually long enough to feel the benefit. If possible, relax somewhere quiet and dark with subdued lighting for a further 15 minutes.

3 For the skin tonics, combine the ingredients in scrupulously clean bottles and keep cool.

ROSE HAND AND NAIL TREATMENT

To keep hands and nails looking their best, regular use of a good hand cream and a weekly manicure make a noticeable difference. For the two hand oils listed below, mix the ingredients together and store in dark coloured bottles when not in use.

ABOVE: *Rose-scented hand oil is refreshing.*

ROSE HAND OIL

Massaging the hands daily keeps the fingers and palms soft and smooth, and the combination of these essential oils is particularly suited to drier and more mature skins. Make sure you massage the backs of the hands to protect against the damaging effects of the sun which can cause liver spots.

MATERIALS
mixing bowl
50 ml/2 fl oz/ ¼ cup jojoba oil
50 ml/2 fl oz/ ¼ cup almond oil
6 drops rose essential oil
4 drops sandalwood essential oil
airtight dark bottle

ROSE NAIL OIL

Massaging the base of your nails every day will encourage healthy growth. You can also use this oil as part of a manicure, soaking the nails for at least 10 minutes after you have thoroughly cleaned them.

MATERIALS
mixing bowl
50 ml/2 fl oz/ ¼ cup almond oil
10 ml (2 tsp) apricot kernel oil
5 drops geranium essential oil
2 drops rose essential oil
airtight dark bottle

ROSE HAND CREAM

This fragrant hand cream is rich in nourishing oils and waxes. Two bowls of thin clear liquids when combined together miraculously produce a thick white mixture.

MATERIALS
50 ml/2 fl oz/ ¼ cup rose-water
45 ml (3 tbsp) witch-hazel
½ tsp glycerine
¼ tsp borax
saucepan
double boiler
30 ml (2 tbsp) emulsifying wax or
*   white beeswax*
5 ml (1 tsp) lanolin
30 ml (2 tbsp) almond oil
spoon
2 drops rose essential oil
airtight china or glass pots

1 Gently heat the rose-water, witch-hazel, glycerine and borax in a saucepan until the borax has dissolved. In a double-boiler melt the wax, lanolin and almond oil over a gentle heat.

2 Slowly add the rose-water mixture to the oil mixture, stirring constantly as you do so. It will quickly turn milky and thicken. Remove from the heat and continue to stir while it cools, then add the rose essential oil. Pour the cream into pots and store in a cool place.

OPPOSITE: *'Madame Alfred Carrière' is a beautiful old climbing rose with sweet-smelling creamy-white flowers tinged with blush pink.*

ROSE HAND CREAM FOR WINTER

Richly emollient, this cream is ideal for hands roughened and sore from gardening and other outdoor tasks. It can also be applied as a barrier cream, to prevent soreness in cold weather.

This is a very nourishing cream, incorporating patchouli oil, which is a particularly good healer of cracked and chapped skin. Follow the old country treatment for sore hands by covering them in a generous layer of cream last thing at night and then pulling on a pair of soft cotton gloves. Your hands will have absorbed the cream by morning and feel soft once more. These ingredients make about 475 ml/16 fl oz/2 cups.

MATERIALS

grater
75 g (3 oz) unscented, hard white
  soap
bowl
90 ml (6 tbsp) boiling water
spoon
115 g (4 oz) beeswax
45 ml (3 tbsp) glycerine
150 ml/¼ pint/⅔ cup almond oil
45 ml (3 tbsp) rose-water
double-boiler
whisk
25 drops patchouli oil
glass or china pots and jars

1 Grate the soap and place it in a bowl. Pour over the boiling water and stir together until smooth.

2 Combine the beeswax, glycerine, almond oil and rose-water in a double-boiler. Melt over a gentle heat.

3 Remove from the heat and gradually whisk in the soap mixture. Keep whisking as the mixture cools and thickens. Stir in the patchouli oil, mixing thoroughly, and pour into pots and jars.

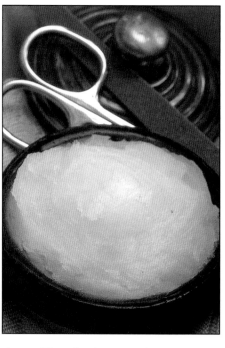

ABOVE: *Winter hand cream with rose water nourishes cracked and chapped hands.*

OPPOSITE: *Hard-working hands will benefit from regular skin care.*

ROSE BATH AND BODY LOTIONS

The Emperor Nero is said to have bathed in pure rose-water and extended this luxury to guests at his frequent banquets, probably contributing to the economic collapse of the Roman Empire! The following simple beauty formulas will not break the bank but are easy to concoct and, when presented in pretty bottles, make lovely gifts.

BELOW: The wonderfully uplifting nature of rose scent makes Rose Body Lotion the perfect accompaniment to any bathtime treat.

ROSE BODY LOTION

This refreshing body lotion keeps well if you pour it into a jar and store it in a cool place.

MATERIALS
mixing bowl
spoon
30 ml (2 tbsp) boiling water
1.5 ml (¼ tsp) borax
5 ml (1 tsp) white beeswax
5 ml (1 tsp) lanolin
30 ml (2 tbsp) petroleum jelly
25 ml (5 tsp) apricot kernel oil
20 ml (4 tsp) unrefined sunflower oil
double-boiler
whisk
10 drops rose essential oil
1 drop pink food colouring
tinted glass jar

1 Dissolve the borax in the water. Melt the beeswax, lanolin and petroleum jelly with the apricot kernel and sunflower oils in a double-boiler. Remove from the heat once the wax has melted and stir well. Whisk in the borax solution. Keep whisking until cool. Then add the rose oil and food colouring.

ABOVE: *Use a few drops of the essential oil to give seashells, pebbles and pumice a pleasing aroma.*

ROSE-SCENTED SEASHELLS, PEBBLES AND PUMICE

Collect seashells and pebbles polished smooth from the effect of waves to make this aromatic display.

MATERIALS
seashells
pebbles
pumice
rose-scented room scent or oil

1 Mix the seashells, pebbles and pumice in a bowl. Add a few drops of rose-scented room scent or oil. The slightly porous surfaces will absorb the perfume and create a soft aroma in a room.

LEFT: *Body lotion scented with rose essential oil is luxuriously relaxing and soothing.*

LUXURIOUS BODY SCRUB

This is a delightful alternative to the loofah, much more gentle and pleasantly aromatic.

MATERIALS
1 tbsp powdered orange rind
3 tbsp ground almonds
1 tbsp oatmeal
90 ml (6 tbsp) almond oil
5 drops rose essential oil
bowl
spoon

1 Simply mix all the ingredients in a bowl when you require it. After a bath, dry yourself thoroughly and rub the mixture into your skin, paying particular attention to dry skin areas. Leave it to dry on the skin and then rub off using a soft flannel.

ROSE-SCENTED TEA AND SUGAR

Scented teas and sugars are simplicity itself but, presented in decorative containers, they are an original gift idea for tea-lovers and keen cooks. Extravagantly wrapped with a box of Festival Shortbreads or Rose-water Biscuits, they make wonderful presents for special festive occasions.

ROSE-SCENTED TEA

The rose petals in this beverage subtly flavour and add a distinctive scent to a high-quality tea such as oolong. This tea, named from the Chinese words *wu* (black), and *lung* (dragon), combines the qualities of black and green teas. The finest blends, known as Formosa oolongs, come from Taiwan and have a rich amber colour and a delicious fruity taste. Pouchong teas are mixed with jasmine and gardenia flowers and you can make your own special blend with rose petals.

INGREDIENTS
200 g (7 oz) highly scented dried rose petals
500 g (1¼ lb) finest quality tea

1 Mix together well in a large bowl and decant into airtight containers, preferably pretty screw-topped jars or decorative tea caddies. Use as any other fine quality tea.

ROSE-SCENTED SUGAR

This delicate sugar has a multitude of uses: it can be used to sweeten cakes and sauces, stirred into cream or yoghurt for a subtle flavouring and substituted for the caster sugar used in Rose-water Biscuits.

INGREDIENTS
20 g/¾ oz/5 cups highly scented dried rose petals
250 g/9 oz/1 cup caster sugar

1 Grind the rose petals in a food processor or liquidizer, just until they are the consistency of coarse sand, not a powder. You can use a coffee grinder but first make sure all traces of coffee have been wiped off or its strong flavour will obliterate the rose fragrance.

2 Mix the petals with the sugar and transfer into screw-topped jars or pots. Make sure you use only the finest quality rose petals, which have been thoroughly dried.

LEFT: *These beautifully wrapped Festival Shortbreads would make a lovely gift along with Rose-scented Tea and Sugar.*

OPPOSITE: *Loose tea scented with petals and rose-heads, served with Rose-scented Sugar and Rose-water Biscuits would make an unusual afternoon tea for a special occasion.*

ROSE TEATIME

In summer, when garden roses are in glorious abundance, you can use the fragrant petals to make rose jelly to spread on scones with lashings of clotted cream. Less indulgent are delicious rose-petal sandwiches.

ROSE JELLY

This pretty pink jelly can be used to sweeten yogurts or fromage frais, as a condiment with cold roasted chicken and to flavour light meat sauces. This makes 500 g (1¼ lb).

INGREDIENTS
500 g/1¼ lb/2 cups sugar
750 ml/1¼ pints/3 cups water
300 g (11 oz) scented rose petals
175 ml/6 fl oz/¾ cup lemon juice
75 ml (5 tbsp) commercial pectin
75 ml (5 tbsp) rose-water

1 Dissolve the sugar in the water with the petals and lemon juice by heating gently in a large saucepan. Bring to the boil and simmer for about 30 minutes. Turn into a large nylon sieve lined with muslin or use a jelly bag set over a bowl. Leave to drip through overnight.

2 Add the pectin and rose-water to the liquid and bring to the boil until setting point is reached (104°C/ 220°F on a sugar thermometer). Remove from the heat and decant into warmed, sterilized jars. Cover with cellophane circles and seal.

ROSE-PETAL SANDWICHES

These dainty sandwiches make a healthier alternative to cake or biscuits and may be served with a refreshing cup of rose-scented tea or a rose-hip tisane.

INGREDIENTS
225 g/8 oz/1 cup unsalted butter
5 heads scented dark pink or red roses
1 loaf soft bread, very thinly sliced

1 Cut the block of butter in half lengthways and place each half on a dish lined with a thick layer of rose petals. Cover the sides and top of the butter generously with more petals. Cover with a lid or layer of muslin and leave for 24 hours in the larder section of the refrigerator.

2 Discard the top layer of petals and allow the butter to soften slightly before spreading on to slices of bread. Use a heart-shaped pastry cutter to cut out the centre of each slice and add a thin layer of fresh rose petals before putting the slices together to make sandwiches.

RIGHT: A complete rose tea, decorated with 'Black Tea', 'Shocking Blue' and pale pink miniature roses.

ROSE WINES AND PUNCHES

There is a freshness and intensity of flavour in home-made wines and punches that is very rarely present in commercial counterparts.

It is also fun making your own drinks to serve to guests on a hot summer's day. The extra effort you have put into your al fresco party will not go unnoticed. These recipes are meant to be drunk the same day – if making them in advance, keep them cool in the refrigerator.

ABOVE: *The pendulous hips in the centre are* Rosa moyesii, *which has pinky-red single flowers; the black hips are* Rosa pimpinellifolia, *a very ancient Scottish rose, bearing masses of creamy-white flowers; the hips in the trug on the left are 'Frau Dagmar Hartopp', a rose pink, single-bloom flower which grows on a very fresh green compact bush bearing crimson hips; the hips on the right are 'Hansa', large and full with a red-violet colour; the hips in the bucket are 'Scabrosa', another rugosa hybrid, with velvet crimson-mauve single blooms and fat, rich hips.*

Rose-hip wine

Traditionally, hedgerow rose-hips were gathered to make wine but if you do not live in the country, you could grow a hedge of *Rosa rugosa*, a vigorous species that produces exceptionally large, round hips. This rose makes enough wine to fill approximately six bottles.

INGREDIENTS

1 kg/2¼ lb/9 cups rose-hips
4.5 litres (8 pints) boiling water
1 kg/2¼ lb/3½ cups granulated sugar
juice of 1 lemon and 1 orange
15 g (½ oz) fresh baker's yeast

Mince the rose-hips roughly in a food processor, put into a plastic bucket and pour the boiling water over them. Stir with a long-handled wooden spoon. Leave to stand for 3 days, stirring daily. Strain the juice through a jelly bag.

Make a syrup by heating the sugar with the fruit juices. Add the syrup to the rose-hip juice and pour into a fermentation jar. Cream the yeast with a little of the liquid, leave to ferment, then add to the wine. Add more boiled, cooled water to bring the liquid to within 2.5 cm (1 in) of the top of the jar. Fit an airlock and leave in a warm place to ferment. Rack into a clean jar, leave for a further 3 months and then bottle.

Rose-petal punch

Fragrant rose petals can be used both to flavour and decorate modest sparkling wines to create a celebratory punch, perfect for a party on a summer's day. This serves about eight people.

INGREDIENTS

300 g (11 oz) scented rose petals
90 g/3½ oz/⅓ cup caster sugar
105 ml (7 tbsp) framboise (raspberry liqueur)
1 bottle dry white wine, chilled
1 bottle demi-sec sparkling wine or champagne, chilled
extra petals or blooms, to decorate

BELOW: *The roses used to decorate and flavour this punch are the shrub 'Felicia'.*

1 Sprinkle the petals with sugar, pour over the framboise, cover and chill. Add the wine and chill once more.

2 Pour through a sieve into a jug. Add the sparkling wine or champagne. Decorate with rose petals.

ROSE CORDIAL, JAM AND VINEGAR

To make the most of the wonderful array of rose petals in the summer months, here are some inspirational recipes for a delicious cordial, a tasty jam and an unusual salad vinegar, all designed to enhance your guests' table.

ROSE-PETAL CORDIAL

A light refreshing drink to serve at any time of day in early summer when roses are in abundance.

INGREDIENTS
25 heads scented roses
900 g/2 lb/4 cups granulated sugar
2 litres/3½ pints/8 cups boiled or
*   bottled still water, chilled*
½ lemon, preferably unwaxed, sliced
sparkling mineral water
extra petals, to decorate

1 Remove the rose petals carefully from the heads and put into a large pan or bowl, with the sugar, water and sliced lemon. Stir three or four times during a 24-hour period.

2 Strain and decant into clean glass bottles. Dilute to taste with the mineral water, adding fresh rose petals for decoration.

ROSE-PETAL JAM

A delicate preserve for scones with cream. It makes 675 g (1½ lb).

INGREDIENTS
600 g/3 lb/6 cups granulated sugar
750 ml/1¼ pints/3 cups water
150 g (5 oz) scented rose petals
175 ml/6 fl oz/¾ cup lemon juice
75 ml (5 tbsp) commercial pectin
45 ml (3 tbsp) rose-water

1 Dissolve the sugar in the water with the petals and lemon juice by heating gently in a large saucepan. Bring to the boil and simmer for about 30 minutes.

2 Add the pectin and rose-water and stir together. Boil hard for 5 minutes. Test for setting point (104°C/220°F), using a sugar thermometer. Alternatively, put a teaspoonful of jam on a cold saucer and put in the refrigerator for about 5 minutes. Then tilt the saucer and if the jam does not run, it is ready for potting. It is wise to test every few minutes to avoid over-boiling.

3 Leave the jam to cool for 10 minutes and then pour carefully into warmed, sterilized jars. Cover with cellophane circles and seal. When the jars are completely cold, label and date the jam.

RIGHT: Rose-flavoured cordial, jam and vinegar capture the essence of summer.

ROSE-PETAL VINEGAR

This delicately scented vinegar can be used in a dressing for summer salads and, sparingly, in fruit salads. It is also effective as a cool compress, to ease a nagging headache.

INGREDIENTS
300 ml/1½ pints/1¼ cups good quality white wine vinegar
scented red rose petals

1 Pull the rose petals from the flower-heads. Scald the vinegar by bringing it to just below boiling point and allow to cool.

2 Snip off the bitter white part at the base of each petal. Prepare enough petals to fill a cup and put into a large glass jar or bottle.

ABOVE: Rose-petal Vinegar is delicious on salads, either in a dressing or on its own.

3 (Left) Add the cooled vinegar, seal very tightly with a screw-top or cork and leave on a sunny window sill for at least 3 weeks.

ROSE HONEY AND SHORTBREAD

Rose-water is a delightful and adaptable ingredient; added to cakes and biscuits, it gives them that subtle taste of summer.

ROSE-PETAL HONEY

This aromatic honey makes an inexpensive and thoughtful gift and is reputed to relieve sore throats and raspy coughs. This recipe will make 115 g/4 oz/⅓ cup.

INGREDIENTS
115 g/4 oz/⅓ cup pale, runny,
    preferably organic, honey
25 g/1 oz/5 cups scented rose petals

1 Put the honey and rose petals in an enamel pan and boil gently for 10 minutes. Strain the honey while it is still quite hot and put into a warmed, sterilized jar with a tight-fitting lid. When the jar is cold, label and date the honey.

ABOVE: *The rose here is 'Amber Queen', but any scented rose petals can be added to the honey.*

ROSE-WATER BISCUITS

Light, crunchy biscuits that are easy to make and bake in minutes.

INGREDIENTS
225 g/8 oz/1 cup slightly salted
    butter
225 g/8 oz/1 cup caster sugar
1 size 1–2 egg
15 ml (1 tbsp) single cream
275 g/10 oz/2½ cups plain flour
2.5 ml (½ tsp) salt
5 ml (1 tsp) baking powder
15 ml (1 tbsp) rose-water
caster sugar for sprinkling

1 Preheat the oven to 190°C/375°F/ Gas Mark 5. Soften the butter and mix with all the other ingredients until you have a firm dough. Mould the mixture into an even roll and wrap in greaseproof paper. Chill until it is firm enough to slice very thinly. This may take 1–1½ hours.

2 Line baking sheets with non-stick baking parchment and arrange the biscuits on the sheets with enough space for them to spread. Sprinkle with a little caster sugar and bake for about 10 minutes until they are just turning brown at the edges.

FESTIVAL SHORTBREADS

This Greek version of shortbread keeps well for a long time in the delicately flavoured sugar, which may be used up in other recipes after the biscuits have been eaten.

INGREDIENTS
250 g/9 oz/1 generous cup unsalted or lightly salted butter
65 g/2½ oz/⅓ cup caster sugar
1 size 1–2 egg yolk
30 ml (2 tbsp) Greek ouzo or brandy
115 g (4 oz) unblanched almonds
65 g/2½ oz/½ cup cornflour
300 g/11 oz/2¾ cups plain flour
about 60 ml (4 tbsp) triple-distilled rose-water
500 g/1¼ lb/2¾ cups icing sugar

1 Preheat the oven to 170–180°C/325–350°F/Gas Mark 3–4. Cream the butter and add the sugar, egg yolk and alcohol. Grind the almonds, skins and all: they should be much coarser and browner than commercially ground almonds. Add to the butter mixture and then work in the cornflour and enough plain flour to give a firm, soft mixture (you may need a little more flour). You can mix it in an electric mixer or food processor.

2 Divide into 24–28 equal portions. Make them into little rolls and then form them into crescents around a finger. Place on baking trays lined with non-stick baking parchment and bake for 15 minutes. Check the biscuits and lower the temperature if they seem to be colouring. Bake for a further 5–10 minutes in any case. Leave them to cool.

3 Pour the rose-water into a small bowl and tip the sifted icing sugar into a larger one. Dip a biscuit into the rose-water, sprinkle it with icing sugar and place in an airtight tin. Repeat until all the biscuits are coated. Pack the biscuits loosely or they will stick together. Sift the remaining icing sugar over the biscuits and keep them in the airtight tin.

BELOW: (From left to right) Rose-water Biscuits, Rose-petal Honey and Festival Shortbread. The roses in the picture are 'Henri Matisse' and 'Grey Dawn'.

ROSE CHOCOLATES AND CANDIES

For special occasions, such as birthdays and at Christmas, hand made chocolates and candies make a delightfully indulgent gift.
Use decorative boxes or tins to contain the treats.

SWEDISH ROSE CHOCOLATE BALLS

This is a very rich chocolate sweet which could be easily made by children if the rum were omitted.

INGREDIENTS

150 g (5 oz) good quality dessert
    chocolate
30 ml (2 tbsp) ground almonds
30 ml (2 tbsp) caster sugar
2 size 1–2 egg yolks
10 ml (2 tsp) strong coffee or coffee
    essence
15 ml (1 tbsp) dark rum
15 ml (1 tbsp) triple-distilled rose-
    water
40 g/1½ oz/¼ cup chocolate vermicelli

1 Grind the chocolate and add to all the other ingredients, except the rose-water and vermicelli. Make into tiny balls by rolling small teaspoonfuls between your fingers. Chill well. Dip into the rose-water and roll in the chocolate vermicelli.

ROSE-PETAL TRUFFLES

An indulgent treat that demands the finest quality chocolate with at least 60% cocoa solids. You can replace the rose-water with brandy if you prefer a less sweet flavour.

INGREDIENTS

500 g (1¼ lb) plain chocolate
300 ml/½ pint/1¼ cups double cream
15 ml (1 tbsp) triple-distilled rose-
    water
2 drops rose essential oil
250 g (9 oz) plain chocolate, for
    coating
crystallized rose petals

ABOVE: *Keep these truffles in the refrigerator.*

1 Melt the chocolate and cream together in a double-boiler until completely combined and soft in texture. Add the rose-water and essential oil. Pour the mixture into a baking tin lined with non-stick baking parchment. Leave to cool.

2 When the mixture is nearly firm, take teaspoonfuls of the chocolate and shape into balls in your hands. Chill the truffles thoroughly until they are quite hard.

3 Melt the chocolate for coating the truffles in the double-boiler. Skewer a truffle and dip it into the melted chocolate, making sure it is completely covered. Leave the finished truffles on a sheet of non-stick baking parchment to cool, placing a crystallized rose petal on each one before the chocolate sets.

LEFT: *Tie the chocolate balls up in a circle of clear cellophane with tiny pieces of raffia.*

$\mathcal{R}$OSE TURKISH DELIGHT

In the Middle East, these sweets are served with tiny cups of very strong coffee.

INGREDIENTS
60 ml (4 tbsp) triple-distilled rose-water
30 ml (2 tbsp) powdered gelatine
450 g/1 lb/1¾ cups granulated sugar
150 ml/¼ pint/⅔ cup water
cochineal colouring
9 drops rose essential oil
25 g/1 oz/¼ cup roughly chopped blanched almonds
20 g/¾ oz/scant ¼ cup cornflour
65 g/2½ oz/⅓ cup icing sugar

1 Pour the rose-water into a bowl and sprinkle on the gelatine. Dissolve the granulated sugar in the water in a saucepan over a low heat. When the syrup is clear, boil until the mixture reaches 116°C/234°F on a sugar thermometer.

2 Remove from the heat and add the gelatine and rose-water. Return to a low heat, stirring, until the gelatine has dissolved. Remove from the heat, and add a few drops of cochineal colouring. Add the rose oil and almonds and pour the syrupy mixture into a 15–18 cm (6–7 in) oiled baking tin and leave to set.

3 Cut into pieces. Sift the cornflour and icing sugar together and sprinkle on to the cut pieces.

RIGHT: Spear the Turkish delights with orange sticks to keep the sugar mixture from covering your hands.

SPRAY OF ICING ROSES

ABOVE: *This spray of roses could be made in any colour to match your table setting.*

*I*ncredibly realistic, this delicate spray of roses and rose-buds is easily made from the sugar paste sold for cake decorating, using a selection of clever tools. It makes a very definite statement as a cake decoration and would also be a lovely gift, presented in a beautiful box like a corsage.

MATERIALS

100 g (3½ oz) cyclamen sugar flower paste

covered florist's wire, cut into 13 cm (5 in) lengths

small rolling pin

five-petal cutter

dog-bone tool

foam pad (optional)

fine paintbrush

100 g (3½ oz) green sugar flower paste

calyx cutter

set of rose-leaf cutters

cocktail stick

1 m (1 yd) narrow ribbon

florist's tape

scissors

1 Roll a hazelnut-sized ball of cyclamen flower paste and mould it into a cone shape. Bend a small hook on the end of a length of wire and thread it through the top of the cone, until the loop is inside. Leave to dry completely.

2 Roll a small piece of cyclamen flower paste fairly thinly. Cut out rose petals with the cutter and thin the edges using a dog-bone tool, resting the petal on a foam pad or in the palm of your hand.

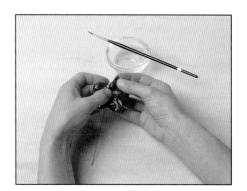

3 Insert the dry cone stem in the centre of the petals. Dampen each petal with water on a fine brush. Lift alternate petals to cling around the cone one at a time. Leave to dry. Then add further petals.

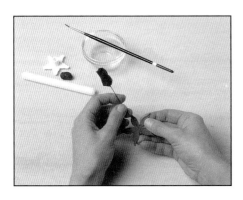

4 Roll out some green flower paste thinly. Cut a calyx with the cutter and thin the edges as before. Thread the wired rose through the centre and fix it with a little water. Roll a small cone of green flower paste and thread it on to the wire, to complete the rose and calyx. Make two buds and three larger roses altogether.

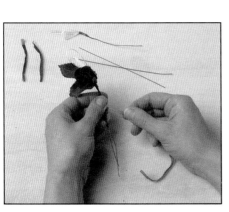

5 To make the leaves: roll out some green flower paste, leaving a ridge down the middle. Cut the leaf out with a leaf cutter and mark veins with a cocktail stick. Holding the leaf between your fingers and thumb, insert a length of wire into the ridge. Twist the leaf, to make it more realistic, and leave to dry.

7 (Left) Wrap a length of ribbon around to make two loops of different sizes. Trim the ends and tape on to a length of wire. Cut the larger loop into two uneven lengths. Make several more ribbon loops in the same way. Arrange a leaf spray, ribbon loop and rose together and tape the stems.

6 Make four large leaves, eleven medium leaves and ten small leaves. Make graduated sprays of three or five leaves and tape them together, using thin strips of florist's tape.

8 Arrange the sprays into a larger bouquet, and tape the stems. Fold the wire ends and tape.

CELEBRATION ROSE AND FRUIT CAKE

This deliciously rich fruit cake is perfect for celebrations such as birthdays or christenings. Covered with a delicately flavoured rose-water icing, it is decorated with whole edible crystallized rose blooms. It makes a 20 cm (8 in) round or 18 cm (7 in) square cake.

INGREDIENTS

175 g/6 oz/1 cup sultanas
375 g/12 oz/2¼ cups currants
175 g/6 oz/1 cup raisins
15 ml (1 tbsp) brandy or very strong
    rose-hip tea
225 g/8 oz/2 cups plain flour
7.5 ml (1½ tsp) ground mixed spice
2.5 ml (½ tsp) ground nutmeg
2.5 ml (½ tsp) ground cinnamon
generous pinch of salt
105 g/3¾ oz/¾ cup butter or
    margarine
105 g/3¾ oz/¾ cup soft brown sugar
2.5 ml (½ tsp) grated orange rind
3 size 2 eggs
65 g/2½ oz/⅓ cup glacé cherries
40 g/1½ oz/¼ cup candied orange
    peel
40 g/1½ oz/¼ cup chopped almonds
15 ml (1 tbsp) black treacle
rose jelly
icing sugar
crystallized rose blooms,
    to decorate

1 Preheat the oven to 140°C/275°F/ Gas Mark 1. Mix the dried fruits with the brandy or rose-hip tea in a large bowl, cover and leave to macerate overnight. Grease and line the base and sides of a 20 cm (8 in) round or 18 cm (7 in) square cake tin.

2 Sift the flour, spices and salt together in a large bowl. In a separate bowl, beat the butter or margarine, sugar and orange rind together until light and creamy. Add 15 ml (1 tbsp) of the flour mixture before adding each of the eggs to the butter mixture. Fold in the remaining flour mixture and stir in the macerated fruit, glacé cherries, candied peel, almonds and treacle.

3 Spoon the mixture into the prepared tin and level the surface. Cover the top with a double layer of non-stick baking parchment with a 2.5 cm (1 in) diameter air-hole cut in the centre. Tie a double layer of parchment around the outside of the tin, so it stands at least 5 cm (2 in) above the rim. This is important as it prevents the cake from burning. Bake the cake on the lowest shelf for 4½ hours; do not open the door while it is cooking. Leave to cool before removing the tin and icing.

FONDANT ROSE ICING

INGREDIENTS

900 g/2 lb/5½ cups icing sugar
2 egg whites
5 ml (1 tsp) triple-distilled rose-water
2.5 ml (½ tsp) lemon juice
120 ml/4 fl oz/½ cup liquid glucose

1 Sieve the icing sugar into a bowl and beat in the egg whites, rosewater, lemon juice and liquid glucose with a wooden spoon. Knead until the mixture forms a firm dough.

2 Spread the cake top and sides with rose jelly. Roll out the icing on a surface dredged with icing sugar.

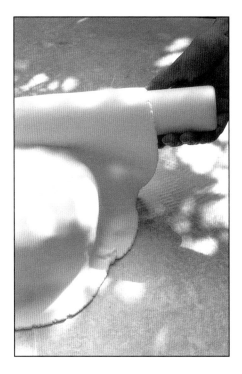

3 Rub the surface of the icing with icing sugar to give an even covering. Use the rolling pin to position the icing over the cake. Cut off any excess. Decorate with crystallized roses.

LEFT: *Gently remove the crystallized rose petals before eating.*

CRYSTALLIZED ROSE PETALS

It is essential, of course, that the rose petals used for any of these recipes are collected from bushes that have not been sprayed with any sort of pesticide and are not growing near a busy road. Pick fresh full blooms carefully, rinse and dry the petals thoroughly, and then remove the white triangle at the base of each petal. When crystallizing complete blooms, leave a short piece of stem to hold them by.

MATERIALS

rose petals or flower-heads
egg white, lightly beaten
paintbrush
icing sugar, sifted
wire rack
tissue paper

ABOVE: *Crystallized rose-heads and petals are a delicious way to decorate cakes and desserts.*

1 Each petal or bloom must be completely covered with a thin, even layer of lightly beaten egg white. Use a paintbrush that gets right into the cracks and crevices and do not forget the undersides of the petals. Any uncoated parts will turn brown and shrivel up. The process must be done quickly before the egg white dries. After the third or fourth rose you will get the knack.

2 Sprinkle sifted icing sugar over evenly and shake off the excess, otherwise any blobs will cause a patchy effect. This may be desirable to create light and shade contrast but a regular and even coating will preserve the roses more successfully.

3 Allow petals or blooms to dry on a wire rack. Stored between layers of tissue paper, the petals will keep for about a week. Do not put crystallized petals or flowers in the refrigerator or they will "weep" – keep in a dry and cool place.

ROSE AND RASPBERRY CHEESECAKE

As well as having rose flavours in your desserts, it is also a lovely idea to decorate your dishes with crystallized rose petals. They add a winning touch to any display.

INGREDIENTS
200 g (7 oz) shortcrust pastry
egg yolk, for brushing pastry
175 g/6 oz/¾ cup quark or skimmed milk soft cheese
5 ml (1 tsp) finely grated, preferably unwaxed, lemon rind
45 ml (3 tbsp) strained Greek yogurt
10 ml (2 tsp) triple-distilled rose-water
15 ml (1 tbsp) caster sugar
350 g/12 oz/3 cups raspberries (or combination of soft fruits)
30 ml (2 tbsp) Rose Jelly (or redcurrant jelly)
crystallized rose petals or blooms, to decorate

BELOW: This light summer tart could be made with a combination of fruits, such as strawberries and red and white currants.

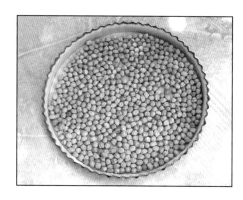

1 Preheat the oven to 200°C/400°F/Gas Mark 6. Line a well buttered, fluted 20 cm (8 in) flan tin with the pastry and prick with a fork. Cover the pastry base with baking parchment and fill with baking beans or dried chick-peas. Brush the edges with egg yolk and bake for 15 minutes. Remove the paper and beans and cook for a further 10 minutes, or until the pastry is golden. Cool in the tin.

2 Cream the soft cheese and blend with the lemon rind, yogurt, rose-water and sugar. Fill the cooled pastry case and spread smoothly. Arrange the raspberries around the edge of the cheesecake. Heat the jelly until runny and brush over the raspberries. For special occasions, decorate with crystallized rose petals or whole blooms.

ROSE PASHKA

ABOVE: *The delicate rose decorations add elegance and interest to this dish.*

1 Heat the cream to just below boiling point. Beat the egg yolks with the sugar until light and foamy and add to the cream. Heat together in a saucepan until the mixture thickens, taking care not to let it boil and curdle. Remove from the heat and cool. Beat the butter until creamy and add to the egg and cream mixture, adding the cheeses slowly then the rose-water, candied peel and nuts. Line the terracotta pot with muslin and spoon the mixture into it, covering the top with muslin.

*I*n Russia, a version of this creamy dessert is traditionally served at Easter, made in a special wooden mould; a simple clay flower pot, washed and scrubbed well and baked in a hot oven for 30 minutes, will do just as well.

INGREDIENTS

60 ml (4 tbsp) single cream
2 size 1–2 egg yolks
75 g/3 oz/⅓ cup caster sugar
90 g/3½ oz/scant ½ cup unsalted butter, softened
350 g/12 oz/1½ cups curd cheese
350 g/12 oz/1½ cups mascarpone cheese
10 ml (2 tsp) triple-distilled rose-water
50 g/2 oz/½ cup chopped candied peel
50 g/2 oz/½ cup chopped blanched almonds
crystallized rose blooms, to decorate

2 Weight a small plate on the top of the flower pot and stand it on a plate in the refrigerator for about 6 hours or overnight. Turn out the pashka by inverting the flower pot on to a serving dish and remove the muslin. Decorate the edge of the dish with the crystallized roses.

ROSE-PETAL PAVLOVA

If you are making ice cream, a delicious way to use up the egg white is to make a pavlova.

INGREDIENTS
4 size 1–2 egg whites
175 g/6 oz/¾ cup caster sugar
60 ml (4 tbsp) Rose Jelly
  (or redcurrant jelly)
300 ml/½ pint/1¼ cups double cream,
  whipped, or fromage frais
300 g/11 oz/2¾ cups mixed soft fruits
fresh and crystallized rose petals,
  to decorate

1 Preheat the oven to 140°C/275°F/ Gas Mark 1. Cut a baking parchment circle and place on a baking tray. Whisk the egg whites until stiff and slowly whisk in the sugar, until the mixture makes stiff, glossy peaks. Spoon the meringue on to the paper circle, making a slight indentation in the centre and soft crests around the outside. Bake for 1–1½ hours, until the meringue is crisp. Take care not to let it turn brown. Leave the meringue to cool in the oven.

2 Immediately before serving, melt the jelly over a low heat and spread it in the centre. Spoon over the whipped cream or fromage frais and arrange the soft fruits and rose petals on top. The dish should be eaten straight away.

BELOW: *Why not make the Pavlova the table centrepiece, by surrounding it with fresh greenery from the garden?*

Index

Aromatherapy massage oil, 66

Art nouveau rose box, 62

Bath and body lotions, 74–5

Black rose vase, 61

Body lotion, 75

Buttonholes and corsages, 22–23

Candle pot with perfumed roses, 32

Celebration rose and fruit cake, 90–91

Christmas centrepiece, 30

Crystallized rose petals, 92

Double-leg mount, 8

Dried rose pomander, 36–7

Festival shortbreads, 85

Fondant rose icing, 91

Gift tags and boxes, 14–15

Hair slides, 46, 50–51

Hand cream, 70
  for winter, 72

Hand oil, 70

Heart and flowers, 27

Luxurious body scrub, 75

Massed rose star decoration, 16

Nail oil, 70

Napkin rings, 17

Olive oil can arrangement, 21

Posies, tying, 9

Potpourris,
  citrus and rose-scented, 24
  rose and delphinium, 24
  summer, 26

Ribbon-rose hairband, 58

Ribbonwork christening pillow, 53–54

Rosa moyesii, 80

Rosa pimpinellifolia, 80

Rosa rugosa, 80

Rose and chamomile facial steam and skin tonics, 68

Rose and clove pomander, 38

Rose and lavender-scented sachets, 42

Rose and potpourri garland, 20

Rose and pressed-flower gift wrap, 13

Rose and raspberry cheesecake, 93

Rose body lotion, 75

Rose candles, 12

Rose cream cleanser and face masks, 68

Rose hand cream, 70, 72

Rose hand oil, 70

Rose jelly, 78

Rose nail oil, 70

Rose pashka, 94

Rose Turkish delight, 87

Rose-bud and cardamom pomander, 39

Rose-hip wine, 81

Rose-petal cordial, 82

Rose-petal honey, 84

Rose-petal jam, 82

Rose-petal pavlova, 95

Rose-petal punch, 81

Rose-petal sandwiches, 78

Rose-petal truffles, 86

Rose-petal vinegar, 83

Rose-scented bags, 40

Rose-scented seashells, pebbles and pumice, 75

Rose-scented tea and sugar, 76

Rose-stamped stationery, 63

Rose-stencilled table-cloth, 64–5

Rose-water biscuits, 84

Satin-rose hat decoration, 56

Scented rose cushion, 44

Single leg mount, 8

Spray of icing roses, 88–89

Starfish and rose table decoration, 28

Stay wire, 8

Stemmed tartan roses, 47–8

Sugar, rose-scented, 76

Summer candle-cuff, 34–5

Swedish rose chocolate balls, 86

Tea, rose-scented, 76

Tudor rose cushion, 59

Two-tone rose scarf, 60

Valentine's heart circlet, 18

Velvet rose coat hanger, 52

Wiring cut roses, 8–9